Credit*Bytes*™

A Selection of the Best Credit and Collection
Articles from the Credit*Bytes*™ Newsletter

By

Lou Figueroa

President

Credit Decisions International, Ltd.

An Important Message to Our Readers

Credit*Bytes*™ is published by Credit Decisions International, Ltd. (CDI) and is intended to share information and ideas that may be of value to credit and collection professionals. CDI is not engaged in providing legal advice and suggests professional consultation on issues requiring legal or accounting opinions.

A Special Thanks

Over the past several years since I began publishing the Credit*Bytes*™ newsletter, many of the topics I've written about have come from the day-to-day experiences, challenges, and issues related to claims received from thousands of clients over time. To all of my clients, I would like to express my heartfelt appreciation and thanks for letting Credit Decisions International, Ltd. support you with your credit risk management and debt collection needs.

To my newsletter editor, Steven Gan, I have become used to your strict scheduling and greatly appreciate the eagle-eye editing and tweaking of each article. It's always a pleasure analyzing each topic in detail with you in order to bring out the best ideas and perspectives possible. Your support and encouragement in making this book possible are greatly and sincerely appreciated.

To my staff, associates, family, and friends, all of you continue to be a wonderful source of inspiration and motivation for me. Whether actively or simply cheering on the side lines, each of you continue to play a valuable role in my personal life and in the growth and prosperity of Credit Decisions International, Ltd.

Thanks so much to all of you!

Lou Figueroa

Table of Contents

Acknowledgement

I know this may sound cliché, but I would like to acknowledge my hard working, loving, and supportive parents for the significant lessons they taught my seven siblings and me.

I'm so grateful to my mother who instilled in us that being kind and compassionate is not a weakness. These are attributes she taught us during our early years. She always showed compassion toward others, which seemed to set the foundation for navigating life's maze of human relations. She would say that no matter what happens, as long as a compassionate element stays within us, life's roads would continue to open up.

My father taught us the values of tenacity, perseverance, and to live within our means. As a wonderful provider to a large family, watching him go to work every day and always striving to support us was a tremendous inspiration. I believe my father's determination and dedication is what has continued to drive me to be at the helm of Credit Decisions International, Ltd. for over 30 years. In addition to my loving and wonderful family, there are two more people who in my younger years taught me the importance of several ideas in business.

One of my early jobs was with Orkin Pest Control. As a very young 19 year old, being hired by Orkin as a pest control technician was actually quite a lucky break for me. Growing up in the inner city, there were not a lot of decent job opportunities for high school graduates. I credit this job for teaching me some very valuable skills.

Fortunately, my first manager at Orkin, John Henry Poloko (who has since passed on) was very influential. I credit him with imparting upon me the art of communicating with customers and people in general. An articulate individual, I admired his devotion to providing very personalized service to every customer. His ability to communicate in a warm and honest manner, nurtured all kinds of customers from various backgrounds into long-term relationships.

As I rose up the ladder at Orkin, the branch manager, Vic Charles, was another man of inspiration. A highly motivated and meticulously organized individual, his main goal was to make our office the best branch in the nation. His motto was, "we need to be nothing but the very best of the Orkin family."

Closely following in the footsteps of both of these gentlemen, I have always stressed the importance of total client satisfaction. My goal is to continue to develop CDI and make it one of the best credit and collections agencies in the country.

Forward

Don't you envy those people who have always known what they wanted to do from an early age? For example, while growing up, some friends dreamed from the time they were small about being a doctor, lawyer, or astronaut, and some actually made their dream come true.

However, for most of us, knowing what we want to do usually comes much later in life, and often only presents itself by chance. For me, wanting to get into the collection business and stay with it for almost my entire professional life is not something I dreamed about doing as a small kid. So just how did I get into the commercial collection field, a field that I have come to know and love for over 30 years?

I suppose it makes sense to give you a little background on my life's journey, so you have an understanding of how I arrived to where I am today.

Growing up in Chicago's inner city, my parents moved from time to time to continue to provide for a large family. From the west side, we moved to Wicker Park, then to Humboldt Park, and finally to the Pilsen area on the south side, where I had my first taste of pierogis and gwumpkies in the predominant Polish community in the '60's. This area later became predominately Hispanic comprised of mainly Mexican immigrants.

For those of you who know Chicago, the Pilsen area is not far from Maxwell Street, one of Chicago's oldest flea markets. From the view of an untrained eye, Maxwell Street probably looked like an endless junkyard. But for those searching for bargains in scrap, electronics, and auto parts, Maxwell Street was a gold mine. It was there that as a young kid I learned a few tricks about hard negotiating but didn't have a clue that this skill would someday come in handy as a debt collector.

My first real job as a young person was with Orkin Pest Control. Now I know that many people might snicker or raise their eyebrows at the idea of being a pest control technician, but no matter who you are in life, and no matter what your socio-economic status is, from time to time you're going to have a pest problem. And when pests make their way into your home, you've got to call in the experts.

As a pest control technician, I needed to study a great deal about pest management. Although I wasn't perhaps a genius during my school years, the challenge of learning about a subject that was completely new and different from anything I had ever studied before sparked an element of curiosity that remains with me to this day. Every single day my curiosity encourages me to read and learn about many new ideas and developments within my professional field.

I rose up through the ranks from pest control technician to exterminator, and then to sales manager at Orkin. One day, as chance would have it, a friend introduced me to an opportunity at a new collection agency in the Chicago suburbs. Not knowing exactly what collections was all about, and probably having the same negative image that other people have of pest control, I decided to change careers and join this agency. For the next few years I became a passionate student of credit and collections. Here as well, I rose through the ranks from collector to collection manager. I would train new collectors within my unit who would later be promoted to their own units. As all this was happening, I guess you could say, "I found my calling."

While hard at work during the day, I was able to attend evening classes at Northeastern Illinois University where I studied political science and linguistics. Not exactly subjects that might be of good practical use in the business world but certainly subjects to continue to open my mind. One evening I decided to sign up for a seminar on how to start a business. While sitting through the basics of setting up and running a small business, it didn't take much to convince me that at a relatively young age, I was destined to further "my calling" and in November 1984 I resigned from the agency and founded Credit Decisions International (CDI).

Since that time, growing and operating CDI has been a very rewarding and a great learning experience. Throughout the years I have been tremendously fortunate to work with wonderful clients, build lifelong friendships, and to have opportunities to travel to international conferences and events, participate in forming industry policy, and meet an exceptional number of gifted people from around the globe.

My life's goal is to continue to learn and improve, serve as a positive role model to many nieces and nephews, and simply be supportive of my clients, family, and friends.

Collection Perspectives

Every collection situation can be as unique as every person on this earth. The skilled collector, knowing that everyone is uniquely different, has developed a real insight into the psychology of how to establish effective and trusting human relations with a wide range of individuals from a multitude of backgrounds.

Personal Guarantees:
The Collection Perspective

A signed personal guarantee, simply by its existence, gives the collector leverage. Two to one, the guarantor had no intention, when he signed it, of jeopardizing his personal assets. He may not even remember signing it. The sudden appearance of an agent, the receipt of a copy of the guarantee, often catapults the obligation into first priority position.

Sometimes, however, the guarantor is impervious to the exposure or cannot be found. In addition to the legal requirements and issues, there are practical elements, from the recovery standpoint, that we have found invaluable to the ultimate resolution.

Even if included in the body of the agreement, the guarantor's name should be printed or typed under the signature, a requirement now in some states. So often, the signature line has nothing but a squiggle; there is no way to identify the individual. If a faxed guarantee is not notarized, and a creditor's representative has not witnessed the signing, the fax should include a signed picture ID.

The sales representative or credit manager should verify the individual's relationship to, or his position in, the corporation, although it should not appear above, on or under the signature line of the personal guarantee. A receptionist, asked to sign it as a favor, may be judged to have insufficient vested interest or responsibility to ensure enforceability.

The guarantor's social security number is extremely important, as is the residence address, telephone number, cell phone number and e-mail address. If the guarantor also submits personal financials (the request for financials may be declined, but it never hurts to ask), the creditor also has at least a snapshot of the current financial situation, liquid assets and real property information should there be a difficulty.

This raises another issue impacting the creditor when granting credit on the basis of personal responsibility for business debt: the right to investigate personal credit histories. A Federal Trade Commission (FTC) opinion letter, July 2000, presented an extremely conservative view of the

Fair Debt Reporting Act. The FTC position, clarified by FTC counsel Clark Brinkerhoff in September 2000, actually does consider it permissible for a commercial creditor, considering extension of credit to a business, to acquire a consumer report on a sole proprietor, a general partner or the personal guarantor(s) of a corporation. Mr. Brinkerhoff advised, however, that a specific authorization, clearly worded, legible, part of the credit application, or in a separate document, must be read and signed by the applicant whose personal credit history is to be reviewed.

There are also a few strange twists to state statutes that can scuttle even a well-constructed personal guarantee. Kentucky requires a guarantee to have a stipulated termination date and disclosure of the maximum liability assumed by the guarantor. In Virginia, the guarantee must be a separate document, not incorporated into the application.

A cautious creditor may, as many others now devising defensive strategies, include a provision in the personal guarantee stating that the laws of the creditor's state will govern the interpretation and enforcement of the guarantee – assuming, of course, the creditor's state is not equally eccentric.

"Subrogation" Collections
Separate the Men from the Boys

The topic of this article may look a little dry but taking on insurance collections is one of the toughest and most complicated claims that a collection agency can perform.

In short, subrogation is the act of one party claiming its legal rights against another to be reimbursed for losses. Subrogation often occurs under property and casualty insurance claims when an insurance company pays its insured for damages and then makes its own claim against the others who may have caused or contributed to it. It is the process of ascertaining legal liability of and asserting the financial responsibility to all parties related to an insurance loss.

For example, what if you arrive at your business and discover a fire has destroyed it due to a defective copier that you purchased. Your insurance company would pay the claim and then subrogate against the manufacturer of the copier to recover the monies paid out to you.

Why has subrogation become so important in the insurance industry and how can it benefit you and your company? Subrogation is important because any monies recovered through the subrogation process go directly to the insurance company's bottom line, which can then be passed on to its policyholders in the form of lower premiums. The subrogation process is the insurance industry's way of not only making sure that those responsible for damages are made to accept responsibility and pay for the losses, but also to keep insurance affordable to its customers and society at large.

Professional collectors are trained to handle subrogation claims, which often require a vast knowledge of insurance, law, and even forensics when negotiating the reimbursement on behalf of one insurance company against another. At CDI, our experience in handling a wide range of subrogation cases has deeply enhanced our overall collection ability to handle any kind of very complicated claim that our clients place with us.

Ten Tips for Keeping Your Mental Balance During Collections

Another week and another collection training for several clients who have asked for a few insights into the world of professional collections. Although there are several advantages to being a third party collection resource, I always try to give clients, especially for those who spend quite a bit of time on collections, as much of an edge as I can. It always seems that towards the end of our training, the following ten tips for keeping ones mental balance, as simple as they appear, are particularly helpful:

1. Keep a mirror on your desk and look at yourself from time to time. Do you look tired or angry? Your expression will be an indicator of your voice and ability to communicate positively, encouragingly, and persuasively.

2. Try to take a five minute break every hour or so. You may not think you need it but it's best to take it. Keeping yourself refreshed is important. Grab a cup of coffee, soft drink, or cold water and keep your system hydrated.

3. Never call right away to the next customer after having had a tense conversation. Talk to your manager or colleague about it. Give yourself a chance to calm down and regroup.

4. Try to eat a well-balanced and light lunch. A heavy lunch can make you sleepy and inattentive to what is being said. Fruits and vegetables will always give you a natural energy boost. Also, have a little healthy snack in the afternoon to stave off any hunger.

5. Try to sit up and maintain good posture while talking. Slouching will make you sleepy and less engaged or alert.

6. Make a point of wearing comfortable clothes. Shirts and blouses that are open at the neck will keep the blood flowing to the brain. Ties and turtleneck sweaters can cause blood to get a little

restricted and may cause irritability.

7. If you have a lot of calls to make, try using a wireless headset, which can make calling easier and more efficient. And even if you only have to make a few calls, headsets free up both hands, which makes looking through several papers or typing on the computer much easier.

8. Always make sure you have the proper information in front of you when talking with your customer. Not having sufficient information or documentation will weaken your ability to answer questions properly, cause stress during the conversation, and impede the collection process.

9. Try to keep yourself calm even when the other party is getting hot. Your excitement will only break the line of communication and diminish the possibility of collecting the account.

10. In view of (9), when a conversation, for whatever reasons is becoming out of control, try apologizing for anything that you may have said that upset the customer. It may not even be your fault that the conversation escalated out of control but apologizing may help to de-escalate the intensity of the conversation and help you to get back on track, which is trying to collect an unpaid account.

The 4 Personality Types of Debtors

In the thirty-five years that I have worked in the collection field, I would say that I've spoken with at least two thousand debtors in many parts of the world in the pursuit of collecting commercial delinquencies.

This experience has allowed me to understand how debtors can be classified when confronted with an outstanding debt obligation. There are four basic characteristics/personalities: straightforward, passive/evasive, aggressive, and deceptive.

The Straightforward Debtor is the kind of person that will call you before you call them. They will let you know in advance that there is a problem and that they are trying to resolve it. They will let you know the score so that if possible, your firm can work with them in a proactive way, especially if they have been a customer for a long time. They will also always come to the phone if you call them and will speak to you politely. In other words, they try to maintain the relationship with your company. There are many people who become debtors due to reasons outside of their control but as long as they continue to stay in touch with us and communicate honestly, all we can do is to continue to try and work with them as best as possible.

The Passive/Evasive Debtor is the kind of person who avoids dealing with debt obligations in a fair and timely way. They will be vague as to when and how much payment will be forthcoming. Or, they will break promises to pay without any concern whatsoever. The passive debtor will also avoid all forms of contact because they just can't deal directly with the debt obligation. This can be very challenging since they can never be pinned down to make and keep promises.

The Aggressive Debtor is the kind of person, as the name implies, who goes on the attack. They display a behavior that makes it seem that it's totally the creditor's fault they haven't paid. They are skillful at making you upset with their strong communication style. They may use profanity and yell on the phone. They may also say things to you that are completely untrue that throw you off balance. They will even purposely entrap you to get you to become angry with them so that they now have an excuse to delay payment or not to pay you at all. The skillful credit and collection professional always remains calm and doesn't allow themselves to fall into this trap. If you hear comments from this debtor that make you want to become angry, take a deep breath, remain calm, and try to continue the conversation slowly and in a soft but clear voice.

The Deceptive Debtor is the kind of person who from the start had absolutely no intentions of paying. They incorporate characteristics from both the Passive and Aggressive Debtor types. They will not only avoid calls and other forms of contact but when you finally reach them, they will tell you some complaint for the first time that is completely untrue and outrageous. Several weeks after payment is due they may for the first time tell you of a problem with the merchandise or service. Without any substantiation they will tell you that their customers complained about the product and that they are now preparing a lawsuit against your company for damages. They may tell you the salesman was rude or that there is a problem with the contract. All of a sudden, out of the clear blue sky you are confronted with issues that would normally be mentioned on a timely basis. All the comments are only excuses to maneuver out of the payment obligation. Not really much you can do with this type of person except hand the account to a 3rd party collection professional or attorney as soon as possible.

No matter the country or culture or even the industry that you serve, my experience has taught me that people are people and when confronted with debt obligations, they will react and fall into one of the four categories.

The Top 4 Things Never to Say or Do to an Angry Customer

Every now and then when claims are forwarded to our office for collection, we are sometimes told from the collection or credit manager that the customer was very angry on the phone, either with them or with another person in the company. Then when we call and talk with the customer, we're told that the creditor became terribly angry with them about a particular issue. Although it's always our position that the creditor is right, we also always listen and try to be the mediator and attempt to reduce the tension and attempt to keep the issues from escalating.

Let's face it, we have at one time or another had a situation in which our conversation with a customer became very heated. When you find yourself in this kind of situation, you'll want to avoid the following:

1. **Never yell back at your customer.** Some customers will push our buttons and the natural reaction might be to respond in kind. The only thing that will happen when you start responding in a loud voice, in an attempt to either control the conversation or overpower your customer, is that he will want to overpower you back, with the end result being a total meltdown in the communication. When your customer is yelling, best to speak in a soft voice and at a measured pace, which will hopefully get your customer to calm down. Some personalities tend to display aggressive behavior, and although the original anger may stem from something else, you happen to be the beneficiary of the anger at that time of your call.

2. **Never use profanity.** This should be obvious but these days so many tend to use "four letter words" when they're describing how good or bad the weather is, that it would be quite easy to let this slip out, especially when you're feeling threatened. Even when your customer is using every foul word in the book, responding with profanity will only escalate the argument into a vulgar war of words. This is not to say that you should just stay on the phone and listen while being spoken to in a derogatory manner. Conversely, if you find yourself in this situation, best to just tell

the customer that you will have to hang up and will call back later when they have calmed down. Whether you give it an hour, or a day, you are the best judge of when the follow up call should take place. It even sometimes happens (from a collection standpoint) that the debtor will actually call back and apologize for their behavior and then commence to have a meaningful dialog.

3. **Never interrupt.** When your customer is going off the deep end on a mistake or problem caused by your company, real or not, just let him/her get it off their chest and listen. At some point they will finally take a breath and expect your response. When this pause occurs, take a breath yourself and start out by saying, "I apologize." At that point, it doesn't matter what the reasons are or who's right or wrong, it only matters that you get your customer calmed down with an apology. Most times when a customer hears an apology forthcoming, they in turn will get a hold of themselves and apologize in return.

4. **Never blame or justify.** Even when you know your customer has done something wrong, which has caused the problem they are so irate about, it's best to maneuver away from whose fault it is and concentrate on trying to resolve the problem. Telling your customer that "if you had not done this or that" is only going to continue to strain the communication. It's best to say you'll investigate the matter thoroughly and get back to them in a timely fashion. It's always advisable to confirm the resolution of your investigation in writing and if there is merit, resolve the issue; however, if there are no issues on the part of the transaction, your goal is still to be paid without having to employ a 3rd party.

Those customers who become angry will often regret it afterwards, as there are many factors that might set someone off. However, it's the response to that anger and how we can defuse it that represents a real finesse in one's ability to forge effective communication.

What Some Debtors Will Do to Create the Illusion of Having Paid

In my 35 years as a collection professional, I've seen my share of ploys by debtors who have attempted to fraudulently prove that they have paid or have tried to maneuver out of their payment obligation. Let me share some of them with you below:

- Creating a check for the correct amount but sending it with a copy (by fax or email attachment) of the reverse side of another check from a previous payment to the creditor to try and prove that the check had previously cleared the creditor's bank.

- Sending a copy of the reverse side of a check with several unrelated processing numbers that give the appearance the check cleared.

- Sending a copy of a wire transfer application, which shows elaborate but hard to read confirming bank seals.

- Sending a copy of a check with the payable name slightly different, giving the appearance that the check was not properly processed on the creditor's end.

When the person in charge has left the company, many times a debtor may take advantage of the situation by:

- Changing dates and content on emails that indicate certain agreements, discounts, etc. favorable to the debtor.

- Forging signatures on documents by the people who left the creditor company indicating certain agreements were made.

- Recreating purchase orders that have different terms and conditions.

- Forging documentation that indicate that the goods were returned.

- Announcing an impeding bankruptcy when no bankruptcy exists.

- Forging letters from a law firm indicating that that the company is in receivership.

When customers have reached this type of fraud, from a collection perspective, the usual and only next step is to try and litigate to secure your interest before the debtor is truly out of business. This type of debtor requires your agent to dig deeper and confirm the true identity, contact information, and potential assets of this unsavory character.

Why Working with Your Collection Agency Is Not a "Set It and Forget It" Relationship

For many companies, using a collection agency is sometimes perceived as a turning point on a claim. Once the claim is passed to the agency, the next time you want to hear anything about the account is if the claim has been collected. In a world where we are constantly dealing with yesterday's emergencies, taking the time to become knowledgeable and proactive in your agency's collection activities is not usually where a credit professional wants to spend their time. However, there are some ideas to consider by not "setting and forgetting" your relationship with your agency.

Getting to know each other - Every professional relationship needs time to develop and learn the nuances and quirks that makes working together both challenging and effective. Understanding the collection process and being kept abreast of the status and developments of the collection along the way will create a level of trust and comfort in working together.

Resolving disputes - From time to time there are going to be claims that will be fiercely disputed. When these situations occur, the agency needs to rely on your team to help them sort through the reasons for the dispute, especially ones that are complicated. Most agencies want to avoid pursuing a collection through the legal system due to the added time, costs, and resources to resolve it. Therefore, when a complicated dispute arises, it becomes necessary for all the members of your team involved in the transaction to respond very timely with the reasons, emails, and documentation to refute the dispute as best as possible. Having a good relationship with the agency will support a speedy response that a qualified collection agent can use to try and effectively counter the reasons as to why the debtor will not pay.

Being your eyes and ears - Your collection agent needs to be another set of credit eyes and ears for your company and industry. Many times collection agents will receive claims against the same debtor from different creditors within a given industry. Some debtors will go from vendor to vendor leaving a path of destruction until finally the weight of the lawsuits and other legal action take their toll, and then it's too late to salvage anything. When your agent comes across this kind of situation and gives you a heads up to be on the lookout for these "try to avoid customers," it can be the difference between avoiding a significant write off or standing in line with the other creditors waiting to see if there is any hope of recovery.

The new word in play for the collection industry is ARM (Accounts Receivable Management) - Collection agencies and the collection industry are continuously on the move, evolving and becoming more sophisticated in the service they offer and the technology they use to operate. For example, integrating your billing system into your agent's collection system can make the processing, handling, and collecting of claims into an assembly line process that can bring past due accounts in much more cost effectively. In addition, many agencies are now offering a full line of before and after sales credit risk management products and services (factoring, credit insurance, credit reports, debt purchasing, legal assistance, etc.) that tremendously strengthen the credit risk management process.

When you and your agency continue to work together in reviewing, strategizing and improving your working relationship, there is no limit to the ideas and opportunities available to refine your company's total credit risk management system.

Credit Information

In this day and age, it's so easy to instantaneously find basic information about each of our customers. However, it's the nitty gritty details of a customer's credit worthiness that are often not so obvious and easily found.

The 3 D's of a Good Credit Application

We have often noted that the credit application included, as part of the claim documentation, is very loose regarding the information requested and/or provided. Let me take a moment to give you my thoughts on the 3 D's for having an effective credit application.

Details - I can't stress enough that a credit application should have a sufficient amount of information being requested on it to give you the best picture possible of your new customer. On the following pages is an example of a credit application that probably has more information being requested than you'll actually want your customer to fill out. But when you look at this sample application, are there any items that could strengthen your present application?

For example, not too many applications ask if the organization owns or rents the premises where it is operating. For the most part, this may not yield much value to you if you're only selling a small consumer product to your customer. However, if you were selling a product that would be installed and become a permanent fixture to the premises, you would definitely need to know this information in the event that a lien needs to be filed to protect and perfect your interests.

Due Diligence - Even with all the information nicely filled out, there needs to be a sufficient level of due diligence performed on this information. Although the sales and profits figures are filled in, if the order is large enough, these numbers may need to be substantiated through receiving the financial statements. I realize that requesting financial statements from new customers to confirm credit information is not going to be easy, and often refused, but if you can get them, they will certainly lend another level of comfort to confirming any financial information on the credit application.

This also holds true for understanding the corporate structure and the officers of the company. We have sometimes found in our own research that the president noted on the credit application was not actually the president recorded on the articles of incorporation or other official process documents. As you can imagine, finding these huge discrepancies for the first time during the collection process is not an encouraging feeling.

Decipher - Try to look and read between the lines of what is written, and what is not. This is actually the most difficult part of every credit application evaluation process since many factors have to be balanced together in arriving at an approved credit number. A website is often one of those easy indicators that can tell you a lot about a company. Sometimes websites do not have something as simple as the customer's physical address noted or the toll free number is a switchboard maze in which you can only leave messages. These may or may not be red flags but just because the website address is clearly written on the application doesn't necessarily mean that our prospective customer wants his suppliers knowing too much about his location.

For most companies doing business on credit, especially where large orders can be submitted, a well developed credit application in which the information is sufficiently confirmed and evaluated will continue to strengthen your credit risk management system.

NEW CUSTOMER CREDIT APPLICATION

APPLICANT'S INFORMATION

Date_____

Name & Title of Individual Filling Out Application_____

Company's Registered (Legal) Name_____

Company's Trade Name_____

Address: Building Name _____

Floor or Room No. _____

Street Address 1 _____

Street Address 2 _____

City _____

State/Province/Prefecture _____

Country _____ Zip Code _____

Telephone _____ Fax _____

Mobile _____

Email _____Web Page _____

CONTACT INFORMATION OF MAIN PRINCIPAL (No Abbreviations)

Full Name_____

Birth date _____ Soc Sec No. _____

Address: Building Name _____

Floor or Room No. _____

Street Address 1 _____

Street Address 2 _____

City: _____

State/Province/Prefecture _____

Country _____ Zip Code _____

Telephone _____ Fax _____

Mobile _____ Email _____

TRADE REFERENCES

Vendor 1 _____

Vendor Contact Name _____

Vendor Address 1 _____

Vendor Address 2 _____

City: _____

State/Province/Prefecture: _____

Country _____ Zip Code _____

Telephone _____ Fax _____

Nature of Business Transactions _____
_____
_____

Largest Amount Purchased 2014 _____ 2015 _____

Payment Terms _____

May we contact to verify trade information?   Yes /   No   Initial _____

Vendor 2 _____

Vendor Contact Name _____

Vendor Address 1 _____

Vendor Address 2 _____

City: _____

State/Province/Prefecture: _____

Country _____ Zip Code _____

Telephone _____ Fax _____

Nature of Business Transactions _____
_____
_____

Largest Amount Purchased 2014 _____ 2015 _____

Payment Terms _____

May we contact to verify trade information?   Yes /   No   Initial _____

CREDIT REQUIREMENTS

Credit Amount Requested per Month _____ **Per order** _____

Your Authorized Purchasing Agent (s) _____

_____

_____

Credit Card Information

If payment by Credit Card is acceptable please sign here: _____

Credit Card _____

Card Number _____

Expiration Date _____

Name Shown on Card _____

Would You Be Willing To Sign as a Personal Guarantor on Purchases? Yes / No

Agreed upon payment terms: Net 30 days from invoice date.

The undersigned hereby certifies that the above information is true and correct. In addition to the foregoing, the undersigned promises to personally guarantee and pay for all purchases in accordance with our terms of sale. If at any time the applicant is unable to pay for purchases when due, the undersigned agrees to pay interest computed at 1.5% per month on any past due amount contemplated by this credit application. If it becomes necessary for our company to incur collection costs for any amount due under this agreement the undersigned promises to pay additional collection costs including reasonable attorney fees.

Authorized Signature: _____

Print Name: _____

Title: _____

Date: _____

The Credit Report Mystique

When it comes to obtaining credit information on privately held companies where financial information is often carefully guarded, the quality of the information in a report should be treated with some level of skepticism. As we have often seen, there can be a huge amount of information reported with tons of statistics and analyses included. Although a very busy report can give the reader a perception of comfort as to the quality of the information, it may not tell us what we need or want to know.

Unfortunately, very few credit reporting companies will actually vouch for the information that is provided, rarely clearly stating that they have confirmed the information through several resources. Instead, what is almost always included at the bottom of the report, in small print, is a disclaimer that the credit reporting agency does not take any responsibility for decisions made based upon the information presented.

When we think about a disclaimer, it should make us pause and wonder as to the validity of the information that is provided. In other words, if we were to read on a credit report that a potential customer has annual sales of $10 million and net profits of $1 million (since statistically speaking a 10% net profit is considered extremely good), we might be inclined to grant this potential customer a significant level of credit based upon those numbers.

But the question that should come to the forefront is, how were those numbers received and how were they verified? Did a staff person, CFO, or the President give them verbally over the phone? Were they sent to the credit reporting company in an email? Were they part of the audited financial statements submitted to the credit reporting agency?

To what extent we rely on the numbers in a credit report all depends on how much credit we are willing to grant. If the amount of credit to be extended is significant, then the numbers have to not only be viable but also verifiable. Being able to do so is the underlying key factor that every credit manager needs to bear in mind.

So before purchasing any number or type of credit reports, the major questions that should be asked to the credit reporting company are:

1. How many sources were used to compile the data?

2. Were the customer's financial statements used to support the financial information presented?

3. How current is the data?

4. Was the information on the credit report confirmed by the object company itself prior to being published?

Unless audited financial statements are received, no credit reporting agency can offer a totally complete credit report. However at least letting the credit reporting agency know that you need to have information that is reliable, will be the first step in dealing with any disclaimers.

The Information that Every Bank Reference Requires

As part of the new customer credit application process, many companies will send a confirmation to the customer's bank requesting details on their banking relationship. Following on the next page is my version of a bank reference confirmation form that I feel includes the major items that will support the overall credit risk evaluation of your customer.

Bear in mind that similar to a trade reference, a customer's banker will rarely give out any information that is unfavorable. In other words, if the customer is having a problem, either with overdrafts or in paying back loans, that definitive information probably will not be forthcoming. Conversely, information that is provided by the banker is fairly reliable. The key is to know to ask for it and to get your new customer's authorization to obtain it.

The first section of the form is requesting information on the customer's daily checking account. DDA stands for "demand deposit account," which is the simple banking term for "a checking account." If your customer's DDA balance is less than $10,000 and they are applying to purchase a machine from you for $50,000 then right there you can see that this customer would most likely have a difficult time paying you in net 30 days.

In each section, dates as to when accounts were opened are also a very telling indicator. Years of a continuous banking relationship versus only months, even if balances are quite large, may indicate a red flag.

Term Facilities is another name for "term loans." A term loan from a bank is for a specific purpose and amount, that has a specified repayment schedule and often at a floating interest rate. Term loans almost always mature between 1-10 years. Seeing that term loans have been paid back further indicate the customer's solid credit worthiness. At the same time, large outstanding loan balances, even if being paid on time, could represent a red flag should the customer suddenly find himself or herself in a difficult financial situation.

Please remember that a bank reference, even if it looks solid, is still only one part of the credit evaluation assembly line.

BANK REFERENCE CONFIRMATION

TO: _____

FROM: _____

Bank Name: _____

Account Name: _____

Depository Relationship

Opened:_____

Average DDA Balance:_____

Overdrafts:_____

Satisfactory ☐   Unsatisfactory ☐

Borrowing Relationship

Line of Credit:_____

Opened:_____

High Credit:_____

Low Credit:_____

Current Availability:_____

Covenant Compliance: Yes ☐   No ☐. If no, what violation?_____

Secured ☐ Unsecured ☐

Last Clean Up:_____

Satisfactory ☐   Unsatisfactory ☐

Term Facilities

Opened:_____

High Credit:_____

Current Outstanding:_____

Maturity:_____

Satisfactory ☐   Unsatisfactory ☐

Print Name:_____

Signature:_____

Title: _____

The Pitfalls of an Incomplete Credit Application

 As credit professionals, we fully understand that the credit application is generally the first stage in which we try to understand a new customer's credit worthiness. As much as possible, we would like all customers to take the time and fill out all sections so that it's complete and accurate. However, the reality is that some customers find credit applications to be a hassle to fill out and a barrier to buying a supplier's products, especially when it is urgent.

At the same time, depending upon the size of the customer, the size of the order, and other factors, credit applications may be accepted with some sections left completely blank.

Although it's well understood that letting the lack of some information slide when there's a rush on getting a new customer processed, an incomplete application could have severe repercussions when payment is not forthcoming, there are disputes against the product, or the customer has gone bankrupt. Let's take a look at the following:

The application has not been signed - This is probably the worst omission since whatever has been filled in on the application may in the end have no legal standing. When a customer cannot or does not pay, a signed credit application that clearly outlines the terms and conditions, and other details of the credit arrangement, strongly supports the collection and litigation process. An unsigned application gives a non-paying customer an opportunity to deny the information on the application and try to maneuver their way out of the payment obligation.

The personal guaranty section has not been initialed or signed - The general trend is that most applications have a personal guaranty section that seldom is "voluntarily" signed or initialed by the customer. Unless the credit policy or procedures absolutely require this, it is almost always left blank. In the short term when payments are humming along smoothly, a personal guaranty is not much of a concern; however, several years later when the debtor corporation goes out of business or declares bankruptcy, despite verifying the customer's personal affluence and wealth, not having a personal guaranty prevents a creditor from attempting to seize the customer's personal assets to satisfy their claim.

The customer's bank information is not complete - Credit lines and available checking account balances (also known as the demand deposit account balance) is the minimum information that is often required to be filled in on an application, but often this information is left out. Knowing and verifying if a customer has sufficient cash and credit lines at his bank against the amount being ordered is absolutely imperative.

The credit card information is not filled in - Just like the personal guaranty, this is an item that most customers do not readily or obligingly fill in. When a customer owes a relatively small amount and for whatever reason, is not paying, a creditor should be able to go ahead and charge the unpaid account against their credit card.

The D&B (DUNS) number is not requested or filled in - Every U.S. company that is legitimately registered in its state will have a DUNS number. D&B has an on-line service called the DUNS Look Up that allows you to search, receive, and confirm the DUNS number of a customer. When pursuing a past due account and the DUNS number has not been noted and/or verified, you may find that the customer may not be a legal entity.

As with many situations, there's a tendency to gloss over the small but important details in order to quickly obtain the greater good; this same idea applies to a credit application. At the time of making an important and urgent sale to a new or existing customer, the repercussions of having an incomplete application will usually become apparent when payment is not being made.

Credit Risk Management Perspectives

At the end of the day, the credit risk manager and an investigative detective are one in the same. They both have to find out all of the facts necessary to understand the truth of each situation.

Beware of the Friday 4:00PM
End of the Month Rush Order

To all the credit managers out there: don't you just love when the sales manager comes running up to you at the last minute, on the last day of the month to have you approve a large order on a new customer to desperately fulfill his monthly sales goal and rush the merchandise to his customer? Talk about pressure!

Here you were starting to wind down and think about a relaxing weekend, but now you're faced with trying to get the order approved and still get out of the office on time. Although the seasoned credit executive knows how to normally address this issue, management may encourage you to approve shipment and then conduct your due diligence. So what may happen now is that you may consciously or unconsciously begin to cut corners and miss some important details that could come back to bite you in the posterior.

Just recently, our office received a sizable claim from one of our clients who wrote in the notes, "This didn't have to happen." I called the credit manager to find out more and she explained that at the last minute she was pressured to approve a new order by not only the sales manager but also by the vice president. At the time that she was quickly reviewing the application, the bank reference, the credit references, and the on-line DUNS report, she did not notice something that turned out later to be obvious.

One of the credit references was from a company where the owner had the same last name as the owner of the company who filled out the credit application. That credit reference turned out to be the cousin of the applicant and unfortunately only when the account started to become delinquent is when the credit manager finally took a solid look at the credit reference and noticed the same name. When the credit manager went to the sales manager and told him that it appears the credit reference provided was not very objective, he also was surprised and felt a little duped.

This is not to say that one's cousin cannot be a good person, but chances are unlikely that he would be an objective credit reference. After all, family takes care of family, and will often provide the credit information that is not so reliable, which is exactly what happened in this case.

Had the credit manager been able to perform the credit evaluation carefully instead of being rushed and pressured to approve this new customer at the last minute because of a monthly sales goal, most likely she wouldn't have had to write to me, "This didn't have to happen."

Conglomerates - The Bigger They Are, the Harder They Fall

Generally speaking, conglomerates are huge multinational and publicly traded corporations that either partially or fully own a number of other companies in a wide array of different industries. One of the most well known conglomerates is Berkshire Hathaway, which has been built up over decades through the purchase of companies ranging from jet engine technology to jewelry. The goal of Berkshire Hathaway, as well as many other conglomerates, is to leverage their assortment of companies to avoid the impact of volatile market ups and downs.

Conglomerates can be summed up in one word: diversification. As business cycles affect industries in different ways, diversification results in a reduced level of investment risk and stable total consolidated gross operating profit results. For example, if Berkshire Hathaway's construction related companies have a bad year or stretch, as was the case after the 2008 economic meltdown, the losses from these companies might be offset by other industries related to food or consumer products.

A strategy of some successful conglomerates is to acquire a company that is not so highly rated or even slightly distressed. By investing additional capital, talent and resources from other companies within the conglomerate, the acquired company can be quickly stabilized and returned to profitability. Some conglomerates will have a more aggressive approach to increase their growth and purchase fairly small companies with a very unique technology, and nurture them into innovative technology powerhouses that offer a highly desirable product or service.

Every day that we are using search engines on the internet such as Google, we are using one of the latest and most dynamic multi-media conglomerates in American history. In 2012, the U.S. and European Union antitrust authorities cleared Google's $12.5 billion purchase of Motorola. What this means is that Google initiated its foray into manufacturing phones and tablets with the aim of not only opening itself up to new markets but also providing a way to defend its core advertising business. And like Google, it won't be too long before Facebook has its own bundle of companies, both related and diametrically opposed to its core business, in order to unlock the next billion Facebook users.

The prominent success of conglomerates such as Berkshire Hathaway is not absolute proof that creating and doing business with a conglomerate is always a good idea. Even Berkshire suffered significantly as a result of the 2008 economic downturn, demonstrating that size does not make a company all mighty. In fact, there is the risk that management will keep holding on to businesses with poor performance, hoping to ride out a bad cycle. Ultimately, some distressed businesses within the conglomerate may use up financial resources to the extent that even stable companies within the group could be impacted.

Many times a conglomerate can often be an inefficient, jumbled, and chaotic affair. For the credit manager, conglomerates can be awfully hard to understand. Not only is it a challenge to classify the company into one category, its consolidated financials can obscure the performance of the conglomerate's separate businesses. Even savvy investors spend hours trying to understand a conglomerate's philosophy, direction, goals and performance. In addition, no matter how good the management team is, its energies and resources may be split over numerous businesses, in which the diversification of the conglomerate could actually be its own undoing.

For most small and medium sized companies, the opportunity to do business with a company within the Berkshire Hathaway or Google conglomerate may be a chance to grow in a way that they could not have been previously imagined. And when this happens, the risk to the credit manager is to assume that since their new customer is partly or fully owned by a multibillion-dollar conglomerate, the credit risk is quite low. In other words, if a 100% Google owned business comes knocking at your door, the red carpet will probably be rolled out and very few questions regarding its credit worthiness may be asked.

Perhaps in most cases this will not be a problem but as you will recall from the 2008 economic meltdown, even a few of the best of the best companies, those that were thought of as being built to last, went bankrupt and left in their wake an economic destruction that affected tens of thousands of smaller companies. Although we may be easily impressed with the name and size of a company and its related conglomerate, it's still always a good idea to act prudently. The old adage, "the bigger they are, the harder they fall," holds true.

How Do You Choose Your Credit Manager?

As odd as it may seem, some of our clients find themselves without a credit manager and have reached out to my company for assistance in finding a replacement. This is not an easy request since every company is unique by virtue of its products, services, size, number of employees, and above all the management that is in charge of running the company. Choosing a credit manager must encompass the idea of whether that employee will "fit" the corporate culture and has to deal with the understanding of what a credit manager could and should do for that particular company.

In one basic sense a credit manager should act as the link between helping the company maximize its sales and at the same time safeguard its assets. Helping the company to maximize its sales means that if a credit manager has knowledge of the sales process, and from time to time accompanies the sales person to sales meetings, they will be able to understand the difficulties involved in trying to solicit new accounts and maintain the present ones. I suppose then that one attribute a credit manager should have is the ability to understand the challenges involved in pursuing and maintaining sales, which will in turn influence credit policy. Conversely, a sales person should also try to understand the challenges of the credit manager and the policies of the credit department.

Although we probably understand that a credit manager should have skills such as professionalism, a strong work ethic, and a positive attitude, these are skills needed for every position. However, what is unique about the credit management position is that it can encompass knowledge and experience traversing a wide range of areas and departments within a company. In my view, a credit manager who has experience in operations, marketing, accounting, customer service, logistics, IT, administration, or human resources is one who brings to the position a depth of knowledge for the problems and issues that eventually impact the credit management function, goals, policies and procedures.

Personally, when I am asked to review the credentials of a candidate for credit manager, instead of only focusing on whether the candidate has experience to manage all of the company's credit activities, I am more inclined to look within a candidate's background for some diversity of professional experience. In this way, I believe the applicant's view of the credit function will be balanced, have a greater contribution, and be more supportive of the company's goals.

How Far Should You Rely on Financial Statements?

 From time to time, credit managers will require their new and/or existing customers to provide their financial statements as another step in understanding a customer's creditworthiness. This is usually required when one of the following occurs:

- a new client's requested credit limit is exceptionally large
- there is a significant increase on an existing credit limit
- an existing customer's creditworthiness is in question

Although most customers are generally not comfortable submitting their financial statements, when they are in need of buying from a particular supplier, they realize that providing sensitive financial information is just part of doing business.

From a credit perspective, receiving the financial statements from a customer and being able to rely on them are two different situations. Any document, whether it is a credit report, a trade reference or financial statement, is only as good as how verifiable the information is and how much weight one is willing to impart to it in making a credit decision.

In order to understand how much reliance should be given to a customer's financial statements, we first need to differentiate how the set of financial statements were prepared; i.e., whether it was through a compilation, a review or an audit.

Compilation
A set of financial statements that have been compiled represent the most basic level of service that a CPA or accounting firm can provide to a client. Like the term implies, a financial statement that has been compiled means that the accounting figures have been received from the client and the accountant has merely put them into a financial statement format.

While compiling the financial statements, the CPA does not make any particular inquiries as to the accuracy of the figures or perform any analytical procedures that are generally performed during a review. In addition, there is no confirmation as to the client's internal control, no assessment of possible fraud, nor any other kinds of procedures that may be ordinarily performed during an audit.

In a compilation, the CPA must comply with Statements on Standards for Accounting and Review Services (SSARSs), which require the accountant to have familiarity of the industry in which the client operates, have sufficient knowledge about the client, and note that the financial statements appear free from any blatant material errors.

The CPA issues a report stating:

- The compilation was performed in accordance with SSARSs.

- The accountant has not reviewed or audited the financial statements.

- The accountant accordingly does not express an opinion or provide any assurance about whether the financial statements are in accordance with the applicable financial reporting framework.

Review
A set of financial statements that have been reviewed, provide the reader with a level of comfort, based on the CPA's review that the accountant is not aware of any material errors or modifications that should be made to the financial statements.

In a review, the CPA designs and performs analytical procedures, makes inquiries, and carries out other activities as appropriate. These activities are based on the CPA's understanding of the client's industry, knowledge of the client, and awareness of the risk that unknowingly there may be a failure to identify figures that could be materially misstated.

A review does not examine the client's internal control or make an assessment for the possibility of fraud, which are activities ordinarily performed under an audit.

The CPA issues a report stating:

- The review was performed in accordance with SSARSs.

- Management is responsible for the preparation and fair presentation of the financial statements in accordance with the applicable financial reporting framework and for designing, implementing and maintaining internal controls relevant to the preparation, and performs analytical procedures, inquiries and other procedures, and provides a fair presentation of the financial statements.

- A review includes primarily applying analytical procedures to management's financial data and making inquiries of management.

- Review is substantially less in scope than an audit and that the CPA is not aware of any material modifications that should be made to the financial statements for them to be in conformity with the applicable financial reporting framework.

Audit

Audited financial statements provide the reader or user with an auditor's opinion that the financial statements are presented fairly and in conformity with the applicable financial reporting framework.

During an audit, the auditor who is also a CPA is required by generally accepted auditing standards (GAAS), to obtain an understanding of the entity's internal control and assess the risk for fraud. The auditor also is required to corroborate the amounts and disclosures included in the financial statements by obtaining audit evidence through inquiries, physical inspections, observations, third-party confirmations, examinations, and analytical and other procedures.

The auditor issues a report stating:

- The audit was conducted in accordance with GAAS.

- The financial statements are the responsibility of management.

- An opinion that the financial statements present fairly in all material respects the financial position of the company and the results of operations are in conformity with the applicable financial reporting framework (or issues a qualified opinion if the financial statements are not in conformity with the applicable financial reporting framework).

- The auditor may also issue a disclaimer of opinion or an adverse opinion (where appropriate).

For many credit managers there is a tendency to bypass the accuracy and reliability of the financial statements and instead rely only on the idea that if the customer has submitted a very confidential document then that by itself lends credibility to the accuracy of the financial statements.

The reality however, as you can see from the differences above, is that when a fair amount of investigation and confirmation is not carried out on the preparation of financial statements, the amount of weight given to them, as part of an important credit decision, should be tempered.

In particular, a set of financial statements that are prepared only through a compilation should be considered fairly lightly, since virtually no inquiries as to how the figures are generated and their accuracy are made.

Furthermore, financial statements that are received from overseas customers have many other kinds of accounting classifications that would not be considered in line with generally accepted accounting principles in the US and as such, only audited financial statements by an international accounting firm would be of significant value.

Finally, like every document that is submitted as part of the credit review, the need to verify certain numbers, figures, and other information will depend upon how much credit is going to be provided against how much risk the creditor is willing to accept.

How the Just-in-Time Inventory System Affects Cash Flow

In this age of achieving six sigma efficiency, effectively managing a Just-in-Time (JIT) Inventory System for many manufacturing companies has become as much of an art as it is an operational science.

JIT is a production strategy that strives to maximize a company's profits by reducing work-in-process inventory and its related inventory carrying costs.

The JIT strategy originated in Japan in the 1950s and was adopted by Toyota and other well known Japanese manufacturing firms with excellent results, in which inventory carrying costs and waste were tremendously reduced. Throughout the decades, major manufacturers in every industry have adopted the JIT Inventory System.

In order to achieve JIT objectives, the process relies on signals between different points in the manufacturing process. Each component in the production process informs the production team when to prepare for the next batch of parts and ties this into the inventory levels on hand that are generally to be used within a 24 hour period.

JIT efficiency also relies heavily on a concise manufacturing forecast and a strict coordination of all the suppliers to keep the assembly moving smoothly. In fact, some JIT forecasts are based on complex mathematical probabilities and statistics that help hone in on accuracy of the inventory parts required to be on hand at a specific time of day.

Unfortunately for many small and medium sized companies that are suppliers to large and well known manufacturing companies using JIT strategies, they often need to keep large surpluses of inventory on hand in their own factories and warehouses so that they can provide parts either as per a set schedule or at a moment's notice. Although this often requires large inventory carrying costs and other related expenses, these Small

Medium Enterprises (SME's) are willing to accept this tight situation for the business opportunity of being a supplier to a very well known manufacturing company.

The problem however is that no system is perfect and there will always be calamities, catastrophes, and forecasts that don't meet expectations, and general problems that can stop a JIT inventory system right in its tracks. When problems do occur, whether the SME is the source or not, the leverage that the large manufacturing customer usually has over the SME requires it to accommodate the problem by:

- taking inventory back
- discounting for delays
- discounting for shortages
- extending payments terms
- not charging interest on past dues

The result is that although in theory the JIT system that the large manufacturing company has implemented is supposed to translate into a cost efficient and effective flow of inventory for all parties, the reality is that for SME suppliers, it can be a cash flow roller coaster.

For the credit manager, who is working at a company that is a supplier within a JIT inventory manufacturing process, understanding these sudden cash flow peaks and valleys and how they can affect a collection forecast will be imperative in supporting their company's financial viability.

How to Get a Handle on Deductions

For many companies, deductions continue to be a serious problem that are costly, cause confusion, and impact customer relationships. Usually the reasons for deductions fall into one of the following categories:

- pricing errors between the invoice and the purchase order or contract

- quantity errors between what has been shipped and what has been received

- special handling costs such as bank fees, extended warehousing, repairs to damaged goods, and any other costs incurred outside of what was perceived to be initially agreed upon between the creditor and customer

In addition, credit and accounting managers are often at the forefront of trying to resolve payment shortfalls, which often show up on aging reports affecting DSO and other credit and collection standards.

Whatever the reason, deductions impact a company in the following ways:

1. First and foremost, deductions impact cash flow and revenues (This is especially true in the retail industry where profit margins are already slim to begin with and payment terms from major customers can be well over 60 days).

2. The time to investigate and resolve deductions is also another expense that not only negates the additional income that may be recouped in resolving the problem, but could actually exacerbate the loss when the deduction is not recouped.

3. Since some deductions are too small to invest time in to resolve on an individual basis, many creditors will simply write them off as the cost of the transaction. However, some companies experience thousands of billings that can produce thousands of very small deductions, which end up being a huge amount of lost revenue.

In view of the cost and impact that deductions have on a company, here are some ways that will help minimize the number and amount of unauthorized discounts:

1. Meet with the major customers who comprise a substantial portion of the deductions and try to ascertain where the problems are coming from resulting in the deductions being taken in the first place. By spending the time to understand and analyze your major customers' internal receiving and payable processes, and then comparing that to your own contracting, billing, packaging, shipping, and associated operations, you will begin to understand where the gaps are that result in causing deductions.

2. Develop a returns policy that is very clearly conveyed to your customers. Most sales discussions shy away from the idea that there will be merchandise that needs to be returned. However, the reality is that from time to time some product may get through that is substandard or not in line with what was ordered or shipped.

3. It would be highly beneficial to establish a Returns Management Team (RMT), which would include personnel from sales, warehousing, logistics, accounts receivable, and other associated departments. This team would implement the returns policy, improve the returns process, and maximize asset recovery. Establishing an RMT would also require investing in technology to support the smooth reversal of all transactions involved.

4. Consider outsourcing the role of the RMT. Some major transportation carriers such as UPS can actually act in the role of your RMT to carry out your returns policy and resolve the return issues. This can be a huge outsourcing convenience, especially for many small to mid-size companies, which do not have the resources and budget to establish and operate their own RMT.

5. Establish a zero deductions goal. In order to attain this goal you will need to continue to clarify, categorize and analyze the reasons why products are either being returned or other reasons resulting in deductions being taken. As you isolate each issue causing the deduction, you will need to adjust your internal controls and

operation to correct the problem, and discuss the corrections with your customer as required.

6. Develop a detailed Return Asset Recovery Program stipulating how returns are to be processed (repackaged, donated to charity, repaired, resold in secondary markets, destroyed, returned to manufacturer, etc.). Salvaging returns at many levels can help to greatly defray the costs incurred in the original deduction.

Although customer deductions are a serious and growing problem for many companies, with a very proactive approach, their impact can be significantly reduced and minimized.

Knowing When to Perform Background Checks on a Customer's Executives

One of the most common problems that I see when certain claims are placed with us for collection is that the owners of the debtor companies are in financial and legal trouble themselves. In other words, for many small to medium sized companies, the owner's wealth and financial stability is almost always linked to that of the company they have established and operated for many years. Let me give you a short story of one incident in which a background check on the owner of a company helped to prevent a possible payment default problem.

About one year ago a customer, let's call him Alex for the sake of the story, and I were talking over lunch when he mentioned to me that one of his long time customers with whom he has had a very good relationship, was going through a divorce after 30 years of marriage. Alex felt sorry for the couple as he thought they were always very nice and hoped that the divorce proceedings would end fairly quickly. Why they were getting divorced was something that Alex didn't share but I asked him if both spouses were involved in the business. He responded that not only had both spouses worked closely together but that two of the children were in the business as well.

Knowing that divorces can often be ugly, I suggested to Alex to have us perform a background check on the owners of this business in order to try and see if there were any particular red flags of which he should be aware. Our background check uncovered a couple of very key issues that were not only alarming but also put their business relationship into a new perspective.

Here's what was discovered:

1. The couple was being sued by a casino in Las Vegas for not paying off a "marker" (monies borrowed from the casino) for $250,000.

2. One of the sons had been arrested for possession and sale of illegal substances.

3. The husband had been arrested for domestic abuse against his wife and there was a restraining order against him.

When the above information came back, without a doubt it was quite a revelation. Although Alex has been a customer and in business for decades and was a major portion of his customer's overall sales, he really needed to do some soul searching as to how to deal with this information. In the end, as hard as it hurt, the amount of credit that was being offered to his customer was tightened up and was explained in very broad terms that due to several factors outside of his control, this was a necessary step for all customers.

As can be easily understood, personal issues can translate into credit issues, and no one is immune to this. Whenever you hear something of a dire personal issue concerning the executive management of your customer, especially for small and medium size companies where the ownership and the company are tightly integrated, it may be a good idea to have a background check performed.

Looking Closely at Your Customer's Bank Credit Line

As many credit professionals rush to get all the pertinent documentation together to evaluate a customer's creditworthiness, which may include their financial statements, there is sometimes not much thought given to the timing and amount of the customer's bank credit line.

A bank credit line (which can also be referred to as a revolving credit facility) is a working capital loan. These are funds that a bank loans to its commercial customers to facilitate their operation, in which accounts receivables are often pledged as collateral. Your customer may have, for example, a $10 million line of credit with their bank, which means they have the ability to borrow up to approximately $10 million at any given time. The amount borrowed and outstanding under a bank credit line is the amount that will be included as a current liability in the financial statements and used when calculating most leverage and liquidity ratios.

When analyzing your customer's financial statements, it's important to understand how close the customer is to reaching their maximum borrowing point under their bank credit line. For example, seasonal fluctuations go hand in hand with credit line limits and it's typical to see the highest amounts borrowed just before and during the busy season when a company builds inventory but has not yet collected on their accounts receivables.

However, if it's not the busy time of the year and you see the customer being close to the total available on their line of credit, a warning bell should go off. If your customer has borrowed up to their maximum limit during the off season and will not have additional availability on the credit line when they need it, this may be a telling sign that they may stretch out their payments to you to fulfill their working capital needs.

In addition, and if possible, comparing loan amounts outstanding against bank credit lines from period to period will also indicate borrowing and repayment trends.

From time to time you may receive a financial statement that has the loan amount against a credit line classified within the long-term liability section of the balance sheet. This long-term liability classification is sometimes rationalized by the idea that the loan will not be paid down within the next twelve months. However, the problem is that from a cash flow and current asset ratio perspective, it's best to include this loan within current liabilities. In addition, although classifying working capital loans as a long term liability may make the financial statements look better (indicating better liquidity), accounting standards generally dictate that outstanding loan balances against working capital loans be classified as current liabilities.

Other points of concern to the bank credit line have to do with the interest rate on the loan and the footnotes or management discussions. If the borrowing rate is close to the prime rate, we can assume the working capital loan is a standard risk for the bank. Conversely, as the interest rate becomes significantly higher than prime, the risk to the bank or other financial lender will also be perceived to be greater.

Footnotes or management discussions regarding the bank credit line can often be an important point to discuss with your customer. Asking questions about their banking relationship will frequently yield insights as to the viability and credit worthiness of your potential and existing customers.

One Credit Fraud Horror Story from Where You'd Least Expect It

Not too long ago we received a very large claim from a company in which the credit manager was no longer there. The new replacement sent me the claim with all the pertinent documentation such as the invoices, the credit application, and a slew of emails between the collection manager and different parties at the debtor company.

As we read through all the emails, there was one that came from a person at the debtor company via their cell phone that when we looked carefully at the email address, the last name was the same as that of the previous credit manager's. We asked ourselves, could the debtor and the credit manager be related?

After further investigation of the debtor's corporate records, along with personal records of the owners of the company, we ascertained that the former credit manager and the owners of the debtor company were indeed related, in which the credit manager is the son of the debtor company's president. It appeared that the credit manager was authorizing credit beyond what the creditor's normal credit policy guidelines allowed and the credit manager, who was also performing the collection function, was letting his father slip under the collection radar.

As we talked with the creditor about their internal controls, we found out the credit manager reported the past due accounts every month to the accounting manager, leaving his father's unpaid receivable off the report (he would export the A/R data into an excel file and prepare his own report). As more details emerged, the authorization of orders and the non-reporting of the past due account went on for over a year.

Finally the big order came in from the credit manager's father and true to form, the credit manager approved the order, which was shipped out, billed, and ultimately left unpaid. Shortly thereafter, the credit manager suddenly quit the company. When we called to the debtor company, the phone was no longer in service, the emails came back, and letters came back with "no such address." The product had been shipped to a rented warehouse. Unfortunately neither the credit manager nor his father has been found (they'll probably show up sooner or later) and we suspect they sold the product off the market and kept a couple of hundreds of thousands of dollars.

So, depending upon the size and situation of each company, here's a quick list of things that could be implemented to help prevent this kind of fraud at your company:

1. Every order should be automatically stopped if there is an account that has any amount over 60 days and reviewed via the accounting system by two people. Hopefully with at least two people required to view the data, the potential to collude will greatly diminish.

2. Every order should be automatically stopped and reviewed if the amount of the order exceeds the amount outstanding plus the credit limit allowed.

3. Credit limits should not be changed within the system by the credit manager without a manager's on-line authorization.

4. Credit applications should be periodically audited to try and minimize the kind of relationship that occurred in the above scenario.

Hopefully these suggestions will continue to strengthen your credit risk management systems.

Snow, It's Not Just Kids Play

Snow is big business, especially if you're in the snow and winter sporting goods industry. And as high as the snow piles up and as cold as the weather bears down, for many companies the lack of snow and cold is the difference between counting your bonus and liquidating your inventory.

As many of you have heard, and perhaps agree with, the world is getting warmer. Now, this is not an article about the causes of why the planet is warming up, but 99% of all scientists and most talking heads in governments across the world now have concluded that climate change is a fact. Greenland, which has one of the largest ice sheets in the world, will indeed be very green in just a few years. And so if you're not a believer in what is causing climate change, I hope that you'll at least appreciate that the average temperature of our planet is on the rise.

So what has this got to do with debt collection? It should be obvious that many dealers and distributors continue to have winter seasons that just don't quite measure up. Oh sure, there are high expectations at the first snowfall after Thanksgiving when all of a sudden there is two feet of snow. But then comes Christmas and in some parts of the country where people are supposed to be all bundled up in their warmest winter gear, they're walking around in shorts and tank tops.

This kind of weather certainly doesn't bode well if you are a distributor of skis and ski accessories. There has definitely been an increase in the number of claims received at CDI against small retailers of snow and winter sporting goods that have been in business for decades but are not able to weather two seasonably warm winters back to back (winters of 2012 and 2013).

Here in the Chicago area we are having a winter drought. Although it finally rained last week for a couple of days, and then snowed a couple of inches recently, for the most part December and January went by without much precipitation. Now in comparison to the slopes of Aspen, Mt. Hood, or Killington Mountain in Vermont, Chicago might not be your snow destination; but we do have Chestnut Mountain and the Midwest can do a brisk business in cross country skiing when there's lots of snow on the ground and temperatures remain consistently cold.

So what does climate change mean for the snow and winter sporting goods industry? It means that you have to view your customer's credit worthiness not just in terms of their location, but also within the diversity of their product line. This also means that every credit professional has to view credit within a long-term environmental framework and adopt credit policies that are going to hedge against climate change and other unpredictable weather trends.

Three Important Points to Charging Interest and Late Fees

One of the claims that I handled recently had to do with a creditor who performed consulting work for a real estate developer to the tune of $8,500. When the creditor initially drew up the contract, he was smart enough to include a clause about charging interest per month on all delinquent balances. As this claim ended up being sued, by the time a judgment was obtained the amount of interest came to over $2,500. The funds in the debtor's account were ultimately garnished and needless to say, having the interest included, greatly defrayed the collection costs. In terms of the original balance, the creditor was almost made completely whole.

The terms "interest" and "late fees" are used interchangeably. Charging a monthly or annual interest is the same as charging a monthly or annual late fee, where the interest rate is used to determine the interest or late fee. In order to try and maximize your recovery on an unpaid balance, there are three important points to know about charging interest and late fees:

1. You can only assess interest and late fees when this is written into your customer application, contract, or purchase order, prior to commencing with the transaction. Be sure to include the phrase: "Accounts not paid within terms are subject to a ___% monthly late fee." There is probably very little legal validity when notifying your customers of interest being charged when it is written only on your invoices for the first time.

2. Generally speaking, most credit applications state an interest of 1.5% per month or 18% annually in the US, and up to 2% per month on applications in Canada. Some states restrict the amount of interest, and you'll have to confirm this, but you're most likely safe if you keep it capped at a rate of less than 18% per year. There are a couple of reasons for keeping a cap on interest rates:

   - Rates that become excessive can be construed as usury and this could possibly result in a violation of local and federal usury laws.

- Charging high interest gives a less than savory impression to the customer and possibly the business community.

3. Select billing software with built-in templates for charging interest and late fees. The last thing you ever want to do is to sit with your calculator and try to calculate interest on the invoices manually. That said, you'd have to go through the calculation performed by your software at least once or twice so that you understand and can verify how it's being calculated. Interest that is calculated in error is interest that probably will not be accepted as part of your total claim.

Most small business owners dealing with slow-paying customers are happy to just get paid, even at a little bit of a discount. If possible, offering a discount for either full payment upfront or within 30 days is a much greater incentive and can be more effective than threats of interest charges and late fees after the goods are already out the door.

Top 10 Mistakes that Cause Collection Problems

It would be wonderful if everyone simply paid their invoices immediately. However, the reality is that in business, you need to diligently collect and follow up on accounts. Unfortunately, following below are some of the common mistakes that can slow down and hinder the process:

1. **Making payment application errors** - Perhaps the most common mistake is the simple error made by applying payment information to the wrong account or applying it twice to the same account.

2. **Not sending invoices promptly** - Invoices should be sent upon the completion of either the service or the sale of the product. If it is a recurring invoice, it should be sent promptly at the same time each month. Failure to do so delays payment and suggests to the other party that they have more time in which to pay.

3. **Not having a standard policy** - From the onset, you need to have a policy in place (and in writing) that makes it clear when payment is due and what the follow-up steps are for late payment. Make sure the customer knows there is a fee for late payment.

4. **Not having thorough follow up** - Someone from your company needs to follow up when trying to collect payments that are late. This means having the information handy and making repeated efforts to receive payment.

5. **Not updating your database regularly** - Far too many payments are not collected because the invoices went to the wrong address or the business was sold and someone new is handling payables. Collection mistakes made through the fault of your company should be easy to correct by establishing a smooth process for updating all contact information.

6. **Failing to address problems early on** - Often it becomes evident that either the payments are routinely late or that you need to be aggressive to collect from a specific account. In these instances,

you should address the situation early on. Perhaps another payment schedule will make it easier to receive payments on time. Don't ignore such problems in the making.

7. **Accepting the runaround** - It's very easy in business today to avoid calls, emails, and other means of communication. Don't allow a company to give you the runaround. Be persistent and reach the person with whom you need to discuss outstanding payment.

8. **Failing to apply payments promptly** - If you receive a payment and do not apply it promptly and accurately, you run the risk later on of not knowing whether or not payment has been made. This can result in duplicate billing of an invoice that was paid.

9. **Failing to lock in a payment date** - It is worthwhile to try and lock in a payment date early on, in the collection process. This way, if you are still waiting for payment, you have a specific date set and can use that for leverage.

10. **Not increasing the level of your collection attempts** - Each invoice should indicate that payment is late and attempts to collect should become more frequent. You should be prepared to take more aggressive action if necessary. But make sure you comply with laws applicable to collection practices.

What Your Credit Policy Requires for a Credit Risk Management Audit

As many of you already know, one of the results of the 2008 economic meltdown was the strengthening of a federal law coined, "Sarbanes-Oxley," (SOX) which was originally enacted in 2002. In short, this law requires that top management at publicly traded companies must now individually certify the accuracy of their financial information. Under this law the penalties for issuing fraudulent financial activity became much more severe, all in order to compel companies to issue their financial information with honesty, integrity and transparency.

One of the most important sections of SOX is section 404, Assessment of Internal Controls, which deals with the evaluation of controls over the safeguarding of assets, including accounts receivables. This section doesn't only mean that an accounts receivable to a particular customer should be legitimate; but that all the procedures harnessed to create, manufacture, ship, and bill the products to a customer are transparent and properly executed.

As SOX compliance requirements may form the basis for a credit risk management audit, the following general policies, procedures, and controls should be part of every credit risk management system:

1. **How credit is determined to optimize sales**

    - new and existing customer credit evaluation and check list
    - credit investigation requirements
    - credit and sales terms authorization levels

2. **Carrying costs of receivables**

    - implementation of a past due account tracking system
    - timely past due account reporting and follow-up

3. Minimizing bad debt losses

- third party collection support
- bankruptcy procedures
- authorization levels for writing off past due accounts to bad debts

4. Organizing the credit department and containing costs

- organizational chart clarifing positions and responsibilities
- human resource considerations
- budget guidelines

When the credit policy includes the above sections and they are executed with transparency, a credit risk management audit will not only show compliance with SOX but the credit risk management systems will be operating more completely as well.

When Customer Service Doesn't Follow Through

For many of us, calling a customer service representative becomes a necessary activity when the product or service we've received has not fulfilled our expectations. When there are problems, companies will often task their customer service staff or other related individuals with trying to resolve the issues.

Unfortunately, from time to time, some complaints with the product or service just do not seem to get addressed. As a result, the customer becomes not only very frustrated but refuses to pay until the problems are finally resolved. In some cases, to make matters worse, not only is the customer's problem not attended to but the account is actually put into collections and sent over to a collection agency.

As you can imagine, under this kind of situation when we, as collectors, make a call to the "debtor," we often find out that the customer actually acknowledges the obligation and has the volition to pay. However, the debtor would like the creditor to resolve the problem that caused the customer to withhold payment in the first place.

Naturally, we listen carefully, note the problem, and report back to the creditor to resolve it as soon as possible. Unfortunately, we still find that we are continuously following up with the creditor to move forward with resolving the customer's problem. As you can imagine, it is very difficult to collect from a customer when a legitimate complaint or problem is not being addressed.

Although most businesses respond quickly, address issues and are upfront with the agent when a contested case is assigned for collection, authorizing the agent to reach a compromise in lieu of investing more time and resources to investigate the dispute will be more cost effective.

When complaints and problems with a company's product or service are not promptly resolved, the company's reputation and long term viability are often significantly impacted.

When Is a Claim Amount
Too Low to Sue?

At what point should a claim be pursued through litigation is a question that I am often asked. Following below are some general guidelines that we at CDI use in considering whether or not to continue pursuing a claim through the legal system, realizing that every industry and circumstance is unique and warrants a decision on a case by case basis.

Claim Amount: At the low end, probably any commercial claim less than $1,000 may not be worth the cost to pursue through the suit process. The increasing court costs and expense of collection fees, along with the time that you may have to invest by attending a trial or a hearing, makes it difficult to justify the expense.

Identifiable Bank Account: If your debtor has previously paid you with a check and you have a copy of it with the bank account information, that's a huge factor in deciding whether or not to continue to pursue a claim through the suit process. In most cases a debtor will not be moving their bank account to avoid a seizure of that account should an execution of the judgment be required. So even if the amount owed to you is relatively small, even less than $1,000, knowing the bank account greatly increases your chances that some amount is still in the account to cover part or all of your claim.

Location: Pursuing claims overseas presents many obstacles and can be a costly nightmare. First, in almost every foreign country where English is not the native language, all the pertinent documents (contract, purchase orders, emails, invoices) need to be translated into the native language, and may even need to be certified at that country's U.S. consulate as being properly translated. This by itself can be a significant cost. In most countries attorneys who provide legal services on collection cases usually do not work on a contingency basis. Instead they will often charge either by the hour or require a handling fee that can be anywhere between 5-10% of the claim amount. In addition, many attorneys in foreign countries will also receive a success fee based upon only obtaining a judgment, whether or not any monies have actually been collected. Furthermore, even with a judgment it may still be necessary to execute it and this is also another cost. Finally, you may actually have to appear in an overseas court, which would be another major expense. In my view and depending upon the country, if the claim amount is less than $10,000, then suing may not be a very cost effective endeavor.

Credit Risk Management Tools

Every professional has a toolbox by which they can build, modify, and take apart the procedures and systems as needed. As credit managers, your toolbox needs to contain a variety of tools that will increase cash flow, expand sales safely, and minimize the risk of selling on credit.

Certificate of Insurance –
Do You Ask for This?

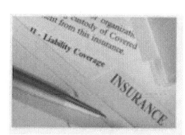

The scenario: Your company has a customer that has consistently ranked in your top 20 for the past 5+ years, which accounts for a significant portion of your annual sales. Recently, the customer placed another large order along the lines of what they've been submitting regularly for the past few years. They've always paid on time and there have been no red flags or rumblings in the market place.

However, one week after the goods were received, you get the news that the warehouse had a major fire, which destroyed all of your product and all of the equipment inside. The cause of the fire was investigated and it was determined that it was a non-arson event which caused the catastrophic damage (arson is almost never covered under any insurance policy).

Although the insurance was enforced and binding at the time of the fire, the maximum coverage of $5 million on the facility and its contents was woefully inadequate against the value of the warehouse, goods, and equipment, which was estimated to be over $20 million. Your goods accounted for $2 million of the total value. This underinsured situation turned out to be not only a devastating blow to your customer's financial health, that eventually led to its declaration of bankruptcy, but also a severe loss that greatly impacted your company as well.

As credit professionals, we seldom think about whether or not our customers are properly insured. Instead we focus on the bank and trade references, credit reports, financial statements, credit industry groups, and other sources that only tell how well our present and potential customers are able to pay us. Sometimes we even do background checks to make extra sure that there's nothing dubious about the company's executive management, but rarely do we consider our customer's insurance and risk management situation to be part of the credit evaluation.

One of the easiest and simplest documents that will tell you about your customer's specific total risk protection is called a Certificate of Insurance. This document provides verification of the insurance and usually contains information on types and limits of coverage, the insurance carrier being used, policy number, named insured, and the policy's effective periods.

In this scenario, if the credit manager would have asked and received the Certificate of Insurance from his customer, in view of the 5 million dollars coverage limit on the warehouse and contents, against the 2 million dollars in goods that were being sold, it may have raised a red flag. Some of the options could have included only shipping the goods:

- to any storage facility designated by the customer, their own or a third party's, which contained sufficient coverage

- in increments with a value that would not exceed a reasonable level of existing coverage on the warehouse facility

- to be named as an "additional insured" on the policy for the amount of the goods being received

- on a just-in-time basis in order to avoid any lengthy storage time in the customer's warehouse facility

We can only begin to think of the options available to us when we realize that there is a problem or risk at hand.

In essence, a prudent credit manager not only understands all of the components of a credit risk management system but also how it fits into a total risk management system. Obtaining a copy of the Certificate of Insurance for the appropriate transactions is one more important step in the process of strengthening the company's total risk management system.

International Factoring - Another Tool in Your Cash Flow Toolbox

By Steven Gan

Factoring is a complete financial package that combines working capital financing, credit risk protection, accounts receivable management, and collection services. It is offered under an agreement between the factoring company (factor) and a seller. Under the agreement, the factor will purchase the seller's accounts receivable. Under a "non-recourse arrangement," if the debtor goes bankrupt or is unable to pay its debts for credit reasons, the factor will still pay the seller. When the seller (exporter) and the buyer are located in different countries the service is called international factoring.

A growing number of companies offer non-recourse factoring services and many of them work internationally. Most factors are either owned by, or associated with, well-known international banking or other financial institutions, insurance companies or industrial organizations. Factoring is now universally accepted as vital to the financial needs of small and medium-sized businesses. It has the support of government bodies and central banks throughout the world.

International factoring is used by exporters who sell on open account or documents against acceptance terms. International factoring eases much of the credit and collection burden created by international sales. By outsourcing the credit function to the factor, exporters can convert the high fixed cost of operating an international credit department into a variable expense.

As commissions paid to the factor are based on sales volume, costs will fluctuate with actual sales, lowering operating costs during slow sales periods. In addition to relieving exporters of the time-consuming administrative burden of approving credit and collecting on export sales, international factoring lets exporters safely offer their foreign customers competitive open account terms. In summary, international factoring provides the following benefits to exporters by:

- increasing sales in foreign markets by offering competitive terms of sale

- protecting against credit losses on foreign customers

- improving cash flow through faster collections

- lowering costs by not having to use letters of credit

- increasing liquidity resulting in greater working capital

- enhancing the borrowing potential

There are also advantages for importers. Until quite recently the Letter of Credit (L/C) was the most universally accepted method to control international trade, in the sense of assuring that the exporter would ship in accordance with the sales contract or the purchase order and that the importer would honor his financial obligations. While this method (or 'term of sale') had considerable merit when goods were moving slowly and at irregular intervals, the L/C places a financial burden on importers, which in most cases is no longer accepted. In summary, international factoring also provides the following benefits to importers:

- purchases can be made on 'open account' terms

- no need to open L/C's

- expanded existing lines of credit

- orders can be placed swiftly without incurring delays, L/C opening charges, negotiation charges, etc.

As the advantages of export factoring have proved to be very attractive to international traders, the number of players in this field has also greatly increased, making rates and fees quite competitive.

The Pros and Cons of Using Skype for Your Credit and Collection Activities

Using Skype or other video conferencing software has become very common for many businesses. Here at CDI we have taken to using Skype and GoTo Meeting for video conferencing with international clients and business partners around the globe. Although many of our U.S. based clients are not setup for video conferencing, the trend is starting to take flight. Some courts have allowed Skype for trials, which although very efficient and a tremendous cost savings, the majority of our court system still requires a face-to-face hearing/trial.

As you can imagine, a voice on a telephone has one kind of impact whereas a face-to-face discussion will have another. Following below are some of the pros and cons for integrating Skype or other video conferencing into one's credit, collection, and business activities.

Pros:

1. When it comes to speaking with present and potential clients, having the tools that allow face time on a regular basis tremendously increases the familiarity of the relationship. When people can videoconference, they can get a much better feel for who you are as a company.

2. Skype and other video conferencing tools such as GoTo Meeting allow one to show files and screens to several individuals at the same time, which greatly facilitates the sharing of documentation and information. Without this tool we sometimes end up having to explain the coordinates (over to the left, under the small title, etc.) of where the other party should look within a document and if it is not readily visible, this can impede the discussion.

3. Skype or other video conferencing software also allows us to easily send documents, links, and images that may be necessary during the conversation.

4. For credit managers who are evaluating new customers with potentially large orders, speaking to the purchasing manager,

controller, or CFO over Skype could give you another level of insight that would not be apparent from just the credit application.

Cons:

1. Our physical appearance may not necessarily match how we sound on the phone. For example, a very low, deep, authoritative voice may conjure up an image in the customer's mind of someone much bigger. Depending upon the customer and the situation, one's physical appearance may work for or against the communication and collection effort.

2. Although talking by Skype with the video turned on allows you to show your facial expressions, it may not help for the customer or other party to see you cringe or wince over what is being said.

3. Skype is developing its own protocol and even though we may see that someone is on line, it's best to send a note first through the system asking if it's alright to talk. Calling without permission may be interpreted as intrusive. At the same time, asking for permission to speak gives the customer the opportunity to avoid the conversation.

4. Although using Skype on a basic level is free, the old adage, "you get what you pay for" holds true. With the free arrangement, Skype can freeze up or suddenly cut off on a somewhat regular basis. This becomes not only annoying but then can give the debtor an opportunity to remain out of contact for a while. However, since Skype's business plans afford a much more reliable level of service, it's worth the extra dollars per month to scale up, especially if you require conferencing a few people in at one time on a regular basis. There are a string of other products, such as Webex, Tango, FaceTime, and other popular video conferencing software that are just as effective.

Like any of the many other tools we use for our daily jobs, video conferencing is another one that can greatly enhance our work under the right situations.

The Pros and Cons of On-Line Credit Applications

In our world of constant technological improvements, it seems that there's not a single item or function that has not been modified or reinvented through internet technology. This is also true for the credit department in which on-line credit applications are being implemented in greater usage.

Like every innovation that can provide many benefits, there are also accompanying pitfalls in trying to streamline the credit application process. Here are some pros and cons to consider:

Pros:

1. When the volume of new customers is high, credit limits are low, and credit approvals need to be turned around quickly, an on-line system would be indispensable.

2. On-line processing increases efficiencies and cost effectiveness for everyone.

3. The data from credit information resources can usually be interfaced into the credit application evaluation process.

4. A credit scoring system can be interfaced to score a new customer's credit worthiness and help formulate credit limits.

5. Bank and trade confirmations can be sent out through the system via fax, or email, which again helps in the rationalizing process.

6. The data on the credit application can be integrated with the accounting management system so that shipments can be released quickly.

7. Shipments can be placed on hold when present A/R balances exceed established credit limits.

Cons:

1. New and important customers, especially those that require "special handling," may find the on-line credit application process uncomfortable.

2. The credit information of a potential customer that is often gained by speaking with the people in charge may be something that is completely lost when an application is processed electronically.

3. There is always the increased potential that data in an on-line credit application will be leaked, lost, or mistakenly disseminated.

4. Signatures on credit applications, particularly on sections such as personal guarantees, may have more legal substantiation rather than clicking the "I authorize" button in the application process, which one could argue was clicked in error or deny it's their electronic signature.

As we move forward in the technology evolution, consideration as to whether or not an on-line application process will work for your company depends upon your industry, the product, the number of applications, and the depth of the relationship required with the customers.

Using Credit Insurance to Strengthen Your Credit Risk Management System - A Quick Guide

We always love hearing from a client, but when a creditor calls to tell us that one of their excellent customers has filed for bankruptcy protection, it is not the call they want to place or we want to hear. When the client says it was completely unforeseen, there are many factors that may have caused the filing, such as the loss of a major customer, a recent large judgment, or the bank closing their lines of credit, just to name but a few.

As there are property and casualty insurance products which help to mitigate against the loss or damage incurred to a company's facility and equipment, "credit insurance" is an insurance product that safeguards a company's accounts receivables.

When a customer fails to pay or goes bankrupt, commercial credit insurance is a product that can help to make a creditor whole again by sufficiently paying out on the unpaid receivable. Following below are some highlights of credit insurance as a viable way to not only protect your company in the event that your customer cannot or does not pay, but to also strengthen your overall credit risk management system.

Firstly, credit insurance in the US is generally offered by about six private carriers and the US Government. The main carriers are:

- Coface Credit Insurance Company of North America
- Euler Hermes ACI
- Atradius Credit Insurance Company
- American Insurance Group (AIG)
- FCIA Management Company
- QBE Specialty Insurance
- Export Import Bank of the US (EXIM)

Coface, Euler, and Atradius are considered to be the top three private insurance carriers and EXIM is the US Government's trade export insurance program. All the private insurance carriers offer credit insurance to cover both domestic and overseas buyers. EXIM is the only program that exclusively covers overseas customers. All carriers try to cover a pool of customers in order to spread the risk of loss.

Factors to consider: Except for government entities, non-profits, and the construction industry, most other companies and industries can be considered for coverage under credit insurance.

There is a minimum a creditor can insure. Coface, Euler, and Atradius have a minimum premium of $10,000 whereas AIG, FCIA, and QBE require a minimum premium of $25,000. It is our understanding that EXIM policies can cover one overseas customer for one transaction and there is no minimum premium.

Here are some pricing structures: In the present market, premium rates can range from as low as .05% and up to .5% against the total annual sales of the customers being covered. For example, if the total number of covered customers has sales of $100 million, the premium rate may be .1% and the premium will be about $100,000.

Most policies contain a deductible and co-insurance, which is the same idea as with auto, building, and other kinds of insurance products. The larger the deductible and co-insurance that an insured is willing to accept, the lower the premium rate will become.

Other important components of premium pricing on a credit insurance policy include:

- industry loss history

- total sales to be insured

- terms of payment offered to customers

- previous bad debt write-offs by the company requesting credit insurance

- aging of receivables at the time the application for which credit insurance is submitted

- the credit management systems, policies, and procedures in place

All the credit insurance carriers underwrite the creditworthiness of the customer in order to establish a credit limit up to which they will cover in the event of a payment default or bankruptcy. In other words, although the insured may require $200,000 of coverage on a particular customer, the credit insurance carrier may evaluate the creditworthiness of the customer only up to $100,000.

Many companies use the amount of coverage being provided as an effective guide to establishing the credit limit to the customer. In this way, a loss will hopefully not exceed the amount of coverage. Broadly speaking, payouts are 75% - 85% of the loss incurred.

Also, many companies that use their receivables as collateral for loans will also insure their receivables. This has the effect of strengthening the financial institution's comfort level, which translates to higher advance rates and lower interest rates.

It should be noted that credit insurance is not all encompassing and may not be a fit for every company. However, it can be one very important product to explore in the event of receivable losses that could greatly impact cash flow and long-term growth and profitability.

General Business

As we plod along in our jobs and careers, the little tidbits of knowledge we gain throughout the years eventually add up to a mountain of expertise.

Are You a Life-r?

During the past several years, CDI has had the distinct honor of being the final stop for four professionals who each retired after serving our company for more than 15 years.

Over nearly 30 years in business, I've been fortunate enough to work with so many caring and long-term team members. Getting to know each of them professionally and personally over the term of their employment has been extremely rewarding. As they retired, each one took with them a sense of pride and many accomplishments during their tenure. On a personal note, each one is missed for their own uniqueness, their sense of humor, talents, and camaraderie with both their peers and myself.

This article is from the perspective of a small business owner who realizes that since there are many special dynamics in every company based upon its size, industry, location, etc., the following are a few thoughts on why I believe members will stay with an organization for a long time.

Hire employees that have the same core values - Look for individuals who have very similar perspectives towards one's work and profession. When considering any new member to join your team, search for a candidate who has a strong spirit and drive to want to work hard and contribute to the organization. This fundamental core value is a precious raw material that under the right circumstances can be developed into a dynamic team player.

Create a positive corporate culture - It is paramount that management set the tone and comfort level for the company. As you can imagine, there are many factors and actions involved in creating a positive corporate culture and there is never one formula; it is as unique as the people within the company itself. A simple greeting sets the tone for the rest of the day. We have found this simple habit to be contagious, since all of our managers and staff not only greet each other in the morning but also upon leaving the office in the evening.

Make everyone part of the team - Every week and every month all the staff and managers come together as is appropriate to discuss various operations, sales and marketing goals, strategies, and activities. When everyone is actively involved and engaged in the company, in which their ideas and input are highly valued, they get excited and motivated.

Be concerned - As the years go by, you learn more about each employee on a personal level, their families, and lives in general. In smaller businesses where each employee's contribution is strongly felt, it is especially important, when someone is not feeling well physically or emotionally, to take a concerned and supportive interest, which will ultimately strengthen relationships. You never know which manager or staff member has had some kind of personal issue where the support of the company was imperative to their recovery. I have truly appreciated when several employees stepped up to the plate to take over many of my responsibilities to keep things running smoothly when I wasn't feeling well.

Give feedback - Honesty is the best policy but it is also very important to be careful about the delivery and the location of the words and ideas. For the most part, although many people may not initially appreciate all the feedback, they still need to have a sincere evaluation of their performance. When a person is trying to offer their best, the feedback that shows what needs to be improved, why something should be improved, and how to go about the improvement, is giving the individual an important road map. When each person understands how to proceed with creating, building, and improving on whatever they are doing, they have a much clearer pathway to achieving their goals.

At the end of the day, everyone needs to come away from their work feeling that they are producing, that their work has value, and that their everyday accomplishments help to move the company forward. This kind of management philosophy we believe will continue to greatly support CDI's long term growth, profitability, and well-being. The longer a team member stays onboard, the greater an asset they are to the company.

Four Points to Shining Through on a Stormy Day

You've just walked into the office and you see your manager standing by your desk waiting for you. As your manager begins to beseech you with the emergencies that need to be tackled by noon, you're also thinking about the other "must do" projects that you have for today, which also have important deadlines. Although we've all been under this kind of crunch before, it doesn't have to stress us out, especially to the extent that what needs to get done, gets done poorly. Take a read through the following points that will help you deal with an urgent and stressful day:

1. **Stop the clock** - Before you can do anything, you need to take a deep breath and make a short list of what needs to be done first, second, and so on. Confirm this with your manager so that both of you are on the same page as to the priority of what the urgent matters are.

2. **Rally the troops** - If the real pressing concerns are suddenly falling on your shoulders then you're probably going to have to delegate a couple of the not so urgent items to one or two others around you. Don't be shy about asking for help, as this situation will actually be a good time to see who will jump in to support you.

3. **Haste makes waste and waste causes work to be replaced** - There's going be a natural tendency to make mistakes as we rush through trying to complete the tasks at hand. Concentrating on the project and eliminating distractions will help to complete the project faster than usual and with less chance for errors.

4. **Follow-up** - We need to confirm that upon completion of the project all parties have received the finished product and all is in good order. Whether you follow up via email, telephone, or in person, it is most important to confirm that all the hard work that has been done has indeed been received in a timely fashion.

So the next time a highly animated and stressed manager greets you as you walk in the door, remember the above four points and you'll sail through the storm and come out shining.

Management's Attitude Can Make or Break a Company

As employees and staff look to management to lead the company, it is imperative that managers and executives understand why their attitudes within the workplace are so important in supporting the success of the organization.

Affirmation: A company's management that adds affirmation and validation to the core values of its workplace will have employees who will react to sudden changes with urgency and care. For example, if there is a constant negative attitude among management, then the announcement of the loss of a major customer will be met with a "so what or I don't care" attitude. However, the same announcement at a company with a positive and affirming management attitude will be met with a sense of disappointment and the urgent need to find out what happened to repair that loss. The overwhelming sense of optimism in the face of negative events helps to affirm and validate a feeling of teamwork that every company needs to survive.

Competitive Spirit: It's human nature to be competitive and a positive management attitude can help foster a healthy competitive spirit. Conversely, a negative attitude by management can grow into almost a cancer like sickness that can cause employees to take advantage of each other for personal or professional gain. In a workplace with a positive management attitude, the competitive spirit is seen as a motivating factor that inspires employees to do the best they can.

Inspiration: Inspiration and creativity are vital for every small business in developing new ideas to grow and to come up with solutions to company challenges and problems. A positive workplace attitude inspires creativity because employees feel that their ideas will contribute to the success of the organization. Conversely, a negative attitude suppresses the creative spirit, as employees do not feel that their ideas, suggestions, and proposals will have any positive impact or even be considered to have value by the management

Loyalty: One of the most promising results of a positive attitude in the workplace is that employees will stay longer and show more loyalty. A positive workplace motivates employees to become vested in the company's long-term development and success. A negative attitude leads to excessive turnover, a lack of cohesion, unnecessary costs in terms of hiring and training, and an atmosphere of "here today, gone tomorrow."

My Many Past, Present, and Future Resolutions

At the end of the year, like many of you, I often make at least one or two New Year's resolutions that I hope to accomplish not only during the next year but to continue into the future. Following below are ten of the many "professional" New Year's resolutions that I have made, remade, and need to make, and perhaps you'll find some of them useful as well. Please read and enjoy:

1. Continue to become more knowledgeable of computer technology as it relates to my business – This is a hard one since I feel that every 10 minutes there's some new technological development that every 8 year old already knows.

2. Continue to become more active in credit and collection industry groups, associations, and organizations – There's never enough time in the year to attend all of the excellent conferences and meetings in our industry. I do have a couple in mind that I will try to go to and participate in.

3. Focus on the passion of meeting new people and forging new relationships – There's no question that in our business, it's the people and the dynamics of the relationships we foster that help to create opportunities.

4. Expand my knowledge base – This one has to do with not only attending continuing education classes in my field but also taking new courses that are outside of my comfort zone.

5. Remain positive and don't sweat the small stuff – As the owner of a business, I have a competing motto that is, "it's the small things that can make or break you." However, I know that if I put the small irritations and inconveniences in their proper place, I'll be a happier camper.

6. Further raise my profile on Social Media – I feel good that this year has seen a dramatic growth in my knowledge and use of

LinkedIn and social media. I've enjoyed connecting with many new people on LinkedIn and participating in several interesting discussions. I hope to continue learning about the various functions, connecting with more associates, commenting on discussions, and nurturing relationships through this medium.

7. Embrace new ideas, especially those that are not necessarily in the credit and collection field – I enjoy hearing new ideas but tend to shy away from them when things get too "unique." Going forward, I'm going to be open to the more "off the wall" ideas only because they may hold nuggets of opportunities that I would normally not think about.

8. Delegate more and empower my team to do more – There's no reason to continue doing the small things; let members of my team take over some of the tasks I often do. Not only will it free me up to take on new projects but it will give them more responsibility and opportunities.

9. Continue to find ways to increase efficiencies and lower expenses effectively – This is par for the course.

10. Keep myself physically and mentally fit – Wish me luck!

11. Finally, continue to meet collection goals and provide my customers with total client satisfaction – What more can I say.

Your Customer's Bookkeeper Just Embezzled Away Your Money

Upon calling a debtor, we may receive the excuse, "I can't pay you (the creditor) because the bookkeeper embezzled our funds and you'll have to wait."

From time to time, some of the claims we receive at CDI have a more colorful background than the usual lack of cash flow excuse. In a recent case that was placed with our office, the debtor, a long-time customer of the creditor was suddenly in a position they never expected to be in. One of their most trusted employees embezzled quite a bit of money.

It was not one of those situations where the individual was handling the accounts receivables, accounts payables, and other cash management functions in which they could easily write themselves checks for very small amounts going undetected over a long period of time. Instead, it was a sudden, swift, and almost guillotine like decapitation of the company's funds, which was well planned by the employee that no one had a clue would ever do something like this.

In short, the trusted bookkeeper, who had access to hundreds of thousands of dollars in the debtor's bank account, transferred funds to an offshore account on a Friday afternoon, flew to the country where the account was located on Saturday, and on Monday removed the funds completely from that offshore account and moved on to another country. As was explained to me, the company and its bank were used to wiring very large sums overseas and so the Friday 3:00pm transfer was nothing out of the ordinary.

Not only was the company financially devastated, but the deceit, moral betrayal, and the planning and plotting that this long term and highly trusted employee went through to perpetrate this crime, is something from which the owners of the debtor company will take a long time to recover.

Although the claim that CDI received against this debtor was over $50,000, our client was not the only creditor; there were hundreds of other suppliers who were also looking for their payments.

As credit and collection professionals, not only are we looking to see what is on a credit application and other credit resources to understand the credit worthiness of new and/or existing customers, but we should often become more creative and ask certain questions that could give us another perspective on our customer's "total risk management system." Within the area of Accounts Payable, here is a list of suggested items to confirm, (verbally or to be included in your credit application) as part of the credit evaluation process:

- Does the same individual perform the A/R and A/P functions?

- Is the issuing and signing of checks performed by the same individual?

- Is the person signing the checks bonded?

- Are checks issued with an electronic signature?

- Are the beneficiaries confirmed prior to any funds being wire transferred?

Perhaps requesting this information as well as requiring a certificate of insurance showing that the potential customer is bonded against employee theft and embezzlement is too invasive to be considered a normal part of evaluating a potential customer's credit worthiness. However, if a new or existing customer is going to occupy a significant portion of your annual sales, then understanding more about their total risk management system will in turn become an imperative part of your total credit risk evaluation.

International Considerations

If you're still not thinking globally, you're missing important opportunities to not only expand your business but to expand your mind.

Brazil's Debt Collection Industry – It's No Carnival

By Steven Gan

One of the outcomes of the economic meltdown of 2008 is that many companies, which relied primarily on their domestic markets, have come to understand that it's imperative to expand into the global arena. As Brazil's economy has continued to steam ahead and become a burgeoning market for many US and Canadian companies, collection challenges and legal issues also arise with greater frequency and urgency.

In order to understand more about the commercial legal environment in Brazil, Mr. Octávio Aronis, Attorney, shares his insights with Steven Gan on the present and future of Brazil's debt collection industry.

Steve: Tell me about the Brazilian debt collection industry, including the number of agencies, collection attorneys, and credit and collection associations.

Octávio: Brazil has a huge debt collection industry comprised of companies of different sizes and specializations. Most of these companies focus on the consumer market. Due to Brazil's expansive territory, leading companies have set up several branches in the major Brazilian states in order to attend to their client base. On the other hand, there are small companies working as collection offices throughout the country. One of the most important Brazilian collection associations is called Instituto Geoc.

Steve: What kinds of collection laws are in place to monitor the collection industry?

Octávio: We do not have any specific legislation. However, it is important to mention that every collection company must have an attorney as one of its partners.

Steve: What was the leading opportunity for you to begin your career in the debt collection field?

Octávio: My brother owned one of the largest collection groups until 1985. By the time he sold his part of the company, he had been looking into international collections and motivated me to get into this business. At that time, I was just returning from my studies at the UCLA Latin American Institute and understood that this could be an excellent opportunity to build on the international area in my father's law firm. I became the first Brazilian member of the American Collectors Association International (ACA), and started to learn about this interesting market.

Steve: At the time you started out in this industry, what was the general landscape of the debt collection industry in Brazil?

Octávio: The Brazilian collection industry used to be solely concentrated in the financial area, whereas most of the American market was and still deals with consumer and medical collections. Another important characteristic is that the majority of collection procedures were taking place in-house. However, this is no longer the case as local companies find it is more effective to outsource to specialized collection groups.

Steve: I think there may be a perception in the U.S. or Europe that the Brazilian culture requires more flexibility regarding payment terms. How do Brazilian's perceive the idea of credit and payment obligations?

Octávio: Brazil has a complex legal procedure. Justice can be bureaucratic, as lawsuits take five to ten years to reach a final judgment and in some cases, even longer. As a result, we always recommend the requisition of credit reports to ascertain a debtor's current legal and financial situation. Furthermore, we find the flexible application of payment terms to be very risky, and do not recommend it.

Steve: In the U.S., credit scores are very important and many people are quite worried about their scores. What is it like in Brazil?

Octávio: We do not have this system yet. However, there is a bill regarding this idea being discussed in our Congress that could be approved in the near future.

Steve: Where do you see the credit risk management industry headed over the next five to ten years, not only in Brazil, but also in some of the other Latin American countries, such as Argentina?

Octávio: Credit risk management is certainly the first step in the provision of credit to any company. New technology has given us many means of obtaining information pertaining to companies globally. In Brazil, and in all Latin American countries, there are specialized groups with relevant information for credit analyses.

Steve: Tell me about your debt collection services.

Octávio: We are a law firm with the capability to handle commercial/consumer claims in all the Brazilian states. Our differential is that we show our clients that we are working together with them and doing our best to solve their problems with professional efficiency, ethics, and economy of costs. Moreover, our attorneys meticulously study supporting documents and make every effort to settle, avoiding long litigation. In the inevitability of a lawsuit against a debtor, we always charge the lowest possible rate in order to minimize additional costs.

Steve: Can you give me a few quick answers on the Brazilian commercial legal system for collecting debts? For example: 1) Are foreign judgments recognized in Brazil? 2) Generally how long does it take to reach an uncontested judgment? 3) What are the costs to litigate? 4) Do foreign witnesses need to appear in court?

Octávio: 1) Yes, a foreign judgment can be acknowledged in Brazil where there is no conflict by each country's respective legislation. 2) It is impossible to predict how long a final judgment may take. As I have mentioned, litigation can take five years or even longer. 3) Legal costs and general expenses are analyzed on a case-by-case basis. 4) Foreign witnesses may appear in a local court; however, there is no obligation to do so.

Steve: What is the one final thought or idea that you would like to leave with this interview?

Octávio: In our years of experience, we have noticed a huge difference in the outcome of an international claim when it has been entrusted to a local counsel or collection agency, compared to when it is dealt with overseas, resorting to long distance phone calls and international notifications. It is the local professional's experience and know-how regarding local laws and peculiarities that make all the difference. This is why we always use international colleagues to process our outbound claims.

Get the Full Name in the Applicant's Home Language

One point of advice I would like to give every business person who is planning on doing business with overseas customers is to always let applicants fill out a new customer application in both English and their home language.   Many times when overseas customers fill out applications, they will use names and addresses based on the premise that an English reader will not be able understand their name or address, even when written alphabetically.   However, when an application is also filled out in the applicant's native language, it will yield details that the English version will simply gloss over.

Let's take a moment to consider personal names.   In many Latin American countries, the family names such as Gonzales, Perez, and Morales are very common.   Applicants may often write the equivalent of their names, or even nicknames, on new customer applications in English only as George Perez or Jim Morales, which really doesn't tell you very much about their true full name.   This is because in Spanish, George is Jorge and Jim could be Diego.

In requiring applicants to write their names in their home language, we will often find that their name is much more involved and contains the mother's maiden name as well as the father's last name, which will help locate and research these individuals should that be necessary.

In French speaking Canada (Montreal), if an English application is used there should also be a paragraph in French that states that the applicant fully understands and has read the agreement completely.   Have them initial this section and of course have them sign and print their full name on the application as well.

Subsequent to receiving an application filled out in both English and the home language, the next step is to obtain a credit report on the company and compare that information on the application already received.   Many times you will find differences between the two documents regarding the contact names and locations, which could be a warning sign to that customer's creditworthiness.   Credit reporting companies that issue credit reports in English can greatly assist a creditor when there is already a credit application filled out in the native language, as they can point out the discrepancies and other points of concern.

The Force Behind East Africa's Credit Reporting and Collection Industry

By Steven Gan

Sam Omukoko is one of the very few people in East Africa who is developing the credit reporting & collection industry. Sam's company, Metropol East Africa Limited, provides credit information reports and collection services throughout Kenya, Rwanda, Uganda, Burundi, and Tanzania. The company is also licensed to provide credit bureau services for banks in Kenya. He is an extremely important link for many international companies doing business in that part of the continent by strengthening their credit risk management safety net.

Steve: Can you give me an overview of Kenya's political and economic landscape?

Sam: Kenya voted in a new constitution some years ago that has ushered in a new dawn for the country. This constitution provides a legal framework for a level political playing ground and has governing structures that provide an equitable distribution of resources.

On the economic front, Kenya has the largest economy in the East African region. The government has set a target to make Kenya a middle-income country by 2030 known as "Vision 2030." Under this program, the economy is projected to grow at a rate of 10% – 15 %. Currently the growth rate is at 4.5 % and is projected to hit 7% in 2013.

Steve: Tell me a little bit about the credit and collection industry in East Africa.

Sam: The credit reporting and collection industry is still in a nascent stage and most collections are currently handled by lawyers who are not efficient. It is made worse by the fact that when collection cases are taken to court, it takes 2 to 5 years and sometimes even longer to get a judgment.

Steve: How many debt collection agencies are there?

Sam: There are two large ones with several small offices.

Steve: Are your collection services similar to other countries?

Sam: I would say more or less yes, but the industry is still young and basic industry standards are yet to be established.

Steve: What are a few of the challenges to collecting that are unique to your area?

Sam: Challenges include tracing of debtors, as the address system is still poor. Many of the debtors are not able to pay because they are not working and as mentioned above, where cases are taken to court, the period to reach a judgment is rather long.

Steve: What do you think will be the greatest impact on the credit and collection industry in your area during the next five years?

Sam: Because we are now a licensed credit bureau, we see a situation where collection effectiveness will increase. Our work is therefore to ensure that we build a subscriber base of credit providers who hopefully share data with us on the credit performance of their customers.

Steve: What would be the most important thing that you would advise to an exporter regarding the business climate in East Africa?

Sam: The five countries that constitute East Africa — Kenya, Uganda, Tanzania, Rwanda and Burundi, formed the East Africa Community, which is both a political and economic union for the peoples of these countries. The total population of the community is about 126 million people with a combined GDP of USD 73 billion. Key industries that provide attractive investment opportunities include: construction, mining, energy, infrastructure, and information and communication technologies.

Steve: How did you start your career in credit risk management? How long have you been in business?

Sam: I am basically a banker by profession. I worked for a major local commercial bank for 12 years before starting Metropol. While working for the bank, I had the opportunity to work in the credit and trade finance departments and also gained extensive exposure in banking operations. I am also a qualified accountant and a fellow of the Institute of Chartered Bankers, UK. This background has given me a sufficient foundation to understand the basics of credit risk management in addition to the fact that I am an entrepreneur. Metropol was established in 1996 and was a correspondent of Dun & Bradstreet for the East African Market for about ten years (from 1996 to 2006). The focus of the business then was business reports but we have since diversified the product range to include ratings and debt management.

Steve: Tell me a little bit about your credit information services. For example, how do you verify credit and financial information on companies?

Sam: When we receive an inquiry from a client, the first place we check is the company registry to establish whether the business is registered or not. We then call the company management and book an appointment to conduct a site verification and interview management on various key aspects of the business. This would cover: operational details, financial information, markets and type of customers plus a brief history of the business. We also do some market intelligence and ask people who are not related to the business what they may know about it. We also use published data and court information that is in the public domain.

Steve: What are the costs?

Sam: Generally a business report would cost anywhere between $100 to $200 (USD) depending on how comprehensive the report is and how urgently it is required.

Steve: What is the time frame required to receive reports?

Sam: We work within a speed of service of between 3 and 6 working days.

Steve: Any last comments or thoughts?

Sam: I must thank you for giving me the opportunity to share some important ideas about credit and collections in my part of the world.

Legal Considerations

I am fortunate to have worked with a large number of attorneys, here in the US and overseas, who have shared their expertise on the laws, regulations, and processes unique to their area.

A Layman's Guide to the Creditors Committee in Chapter 11 Cases

For those of us who are not attorneys, let me take a moment to share with you a layman's overview of the role of an unsecured creditor's committee and its purpose as it relates to the reorganization of cases under Chapter 11 of the US Bankruptcy Code.

Chapter 11 Bankruptcy, a General Description

In most Chapter 11 reorganization cases that are filed, management hopes to bring the business back to solvency and to present a plan of repayment to its creditors. The plan will need to be approved by the creditors and also to comply with the Bankruptcy Code requirements for the Court's approval, or " confirmation," as it's called under the Code.

Unless a trustee is appointed to oversee the business, the debtor will have an exclusive right to file a plan during the first 120 days after the case is filed. After 120 days (unless the Court orders otherwise) the debtor and/or any other party, including a creditor or the creditor's committee, may instead file a plan. There is no requirement (unless a date has been specifically set by the Court on request of some party) that the debtor must file a plan within the first 120 days or by any subsequent date.

Before a plan can be submitted to the creditors, a disclosure hearing is held. At that time, the person or entity proposing the plan must show the Bankruptcy Judge that their disclosure statement provides sufficient information to creditors to allow them to make an informed decision. If the Judge finds the disclosure adequate, the plan, disclosure statement, and ballots will be mailed to all creditors for voting. If the plan is approved by the creditors and confirmed by the Court, payment to creditors can begin according to the terms of the plan.

The present management of the debtor will remain in possession and in control of its business unless the Court orders that a trustee is appointed, the case be dismissed, or the case be converted to a Chapter 7 liquidation proceeding.

Who and what is the Trustee?

The United States Trustee System is part of the Department of Justice; responsible for overseeing the administration of bankruptcy cases and consists of 21 regional U.S. Trustee Offices nationwide.

In CDI's area, the United States Trustee for Region 11 serves the federal judicial districts established for the Northern District of Illinois and Wisconsin. The Trustee's role is to insure that the debtor and its management are operating in good faith, in conformity with the Bankruptcy Code, and that the debtor is making all efforts to bring about an effective reorganization. This is accomplished through financial reporting requirements and other controls placed on the debtor, and in some cases, periodic visits to the debtor's place of business. The Trustee does not represent or advocate for the interests of any particular group of creditors.

The Creditor's Committee

Under section 1102(a) of the Bankruptcy Code, the Trustee has the responsibility of organizing and appointing a committee of creditors holding unsecured claims. The unsecured creditor's committee neither manages the business nor controls the debtor's assets. The debtor in possession (or trustee, if one has been appointed) remains in control. It is assumed that the committee will represent the interests and attempt to maximize recovery for all unsecured creditors in its negotiations with the debtor and other parties in the case. The Bankruptcy Code provides that a creditor's committee may:

- Review the progress of the case with the debtor. As the debtor is required to file periodic financial reports with the Trustee, these reports will provide valuable information for the committee to make certain evaluations and decisions.

- Investigate the financial condition of the debtor, the operation of the debtor's business, and decide whether or not the debtor's business should continue.

- Participate in the formulation of a plan.

- Ask the Court to appoint an examiner in the bankruptcy case. An examiner is a professional (often a CPA) with the expertise to investigate the business and file a report regarding the viability of the debtor, the competence of past or current management, and the possibility of fraud.

- Request the appointment of a trustee to be charged with the responsibility of controlling the debtor's assets.

- Ask the Court to either dismiss the case or to convert it to one under Chapter 7 (liquidation).

The Trustee will appoint committee members. The committee ordinarily consists of those persons who hold the seven largest unsecured claims and who are willing to serve. Generally, at the first meeting of creditors the committee will:

- elect a chairman

- discuss the status of the case

- consider whether the committee's powers should be invoked and if so, which ones

- make plans for future meetings

In order for a committee to be effective in a bankruptcy case, its members must possess knowledge about the bankruptcy process and be committed to working with the debtor to do all that is necessary to achieve the best results possible. Committee members should commit themselves to reviewing the information and issues that are presented to them in an objective and professional manner. Their recommendations and decisions should be based on sound business judgment, designed to move the debtor toward a successful resolution of its problems and challenges.

Serving on a committee can provide a creditor with several benefits that include:

- influencing the direction and the outcome of the bankruptcy filing

- accessing information about how the debtor fell into a distressed situation

- deciding whether or not to consider selling to the debtor on "post petition" open account terms

- notifying management of any post petition invoices becoming past due

While the appointment on a committee does not guarantee that the case will have a successful conclusion, one thing is certain: the absence of a dedicated creditor's committee will increase the chances of allowing the debtor's already distressed financial situation to evolve into a liquidation.

Class-action Lawsuit Against Credit Card Companies Allows Merchants to Pass-on Transaction Fees to Customers

Given the prolonged sluggish economy, credit professionals have continued to look for ways to minimize payment default risks with Business-to-Business (B2B) credit sales and boost cash flow through the use of credit cards. Since customers sometimes insist on using credit cards, even personal cards, to pay for B2B purchases, companies have been struggling with the level of transaction fees eating into gross profits.

As you may know, thousands of companies that accepted payment by credit card for years sued VISA, MasterCard, and several banks that issue cards, contending that the card companies engaged in anti-competitive behavior through price-fixing to charge high processing fees.

Now, VISA, MasterCard and the nation's biggest banks will begin paying close to $7 billion to merchants to end a seven year dispute over credit card interchange fees (also known as a surcharge, convenience fee or transaction fee). The lawsuit was brought about by claims that merchants paid excessive fees to accept VISA and MasterCard during the period January 1, 2004 to November 28, 2012. The settlement includes at least $6 billion in payments to 7 million merchants for past damages and a temporary reduction in interchange fees valued at $1.2 billion.

The lawsuit brought changes to what is called the "Rule Changes Settlement Class" and includes all persons, businesses, and other entities that accept VISA or MasterCard in the US after November 28, 2012.

The highlights of these changes are as follows:

- Since January 27, 2013, merchants are now able to charge an extra fee or pass on a surcharge to customers, whether commercial or consumer, who pay with a VISA or MasterCard.

- Merchants must disclose to all of their customers that they have instituted a formal program to pass on the surcharge fee.

- The surcharge fee can only be applied once. For example, if you have a customer that owes $10,000 and you have an agreement to accept payments at the rate of $1,000 per week, the fee can only be imposed on the first payment and not on the remaining consecutive payments for the same purchase.

- Merchants may only pass on the surcharge fee to the extent that their bank or credit card company is charging them.

- The surcharge must be the same for all VISA credit cards or all MasterCard credit cards and cannot be applied to Debit card transactions.

- Merchants may now impose a surcharge on a particular VISA or MasterCard product, such as VISA Reward or Signature cards.

- Merchants are now able to offer discounts or other financial incentives at the point of sale to customers who pay with an alternative payment form.

- Merchants are now allowed to set a $10 minimum purchase for VISA and MasterCard transactions.

- There are still eleven states that have anti-surcharge laws and these include: California, Colorado, Connecticut, Florida, Kansas, Maine, Massachusetts, New York, Oklahoma, Texas, and Utah (Wisconsin will not be prohibited as long as the fee is under $25). The aim of the anti-surcharge law is to protect consumers from being charged the transaction fees from the largest retailers like Walmart and Target.

- There are twenty states that are also contemplating anti-surcharge laws.

- Canadian customers who do business in the US in which they are billed in US dollars can be subject to a merchant's surcharge program.

Although Amex and Discover were not sued, they have indicated that they are in-line with the changes in the new law.

The latter represents a quick summary of the new law regarding transaction fees but it is highly recommended that prior to implementing a formal program that you consult with your attorney accordingly.

Counterclaims - Beware of the Misunderstandings

 The final step in the collection process on a commercial delinquency is the filing of a suit against the debtor. Generally, although every effort is taken to avoid this step, it's one of the last tools in any collection entity's collection arsenal.

For the most part, here in the US when collection agencies and collection attorneys initially accept a claim for collection, the commission rate is usually presented to the creditor in two stages; pre-suit and post-suit, in which the difference generally ranges from an additional 5-10%. For example, a pre-suit commission rate may be 25% and a post-suit commission rate may be about 35%. It all depends upon the agency, attorney, amount of the claim, and the length of time outstanding.

In addition to the post-suit commission rate, creditors are informed of the additional legal costs to pursue litigation, which includes court costs to process the claim as well as a request for a non-contingent suit fee, which in some instances might be anywhere from 2.5% to as high as 10% of the amount of the claim. A good agency will have an agreement with the various law firms to waive these hefty non-contingent suit fees and handle suits by advancing court costs only. In most cases, the time that an attorney spends on the claim is not charged to the creditor and is covered under a post-suit contingency commission rate. Should the lawsuit materialize into a judgment on the creditor's behalf that still cannot be fulfilled, the attorney will not charge for the time incurred to pursue the claim.

One of the most prevalent strategies of a debtor upon being sued is to hire an attorney and file a counterclaim against the creditor. There are many legitimate reasons why a debtor may file a counterclaim and a few of them are as follows:

- The goods or services were defective.

- The creditor did not uphold certain contractual obligations such as a warranty.

- The contract was already legally cancelled.

- The creditor's lack of contractual fulfillment caused damages to be incurred.

- The creditor caused damage to the debtor's location and facility.

- The contract violated certain municipal, state, or federal statutes making the contract unenforceable.

Bear in mind that not every counterclaim is based upon a legitimate complaint by the debtor against the creditor. In fact, most countersuits are based upon unsubstantiated claims as a strategy to maneuver out of the original debt obligation. If for example, an unpaid $10,000 claim is sued and is suddenly thwarted by a $20,000 counterclaim, this may be sufficient action by the debtor to force the creditor to drop their original claim.

For whatever the reasons of a debtor's motive to file a counterclaim, the attorney representing the creditor in the suit against the debtor must now in turn defend the creditor. In this case the commission and out of pocket expenses charged in the original lawsuit against the debtor will not apply in defending the same creditor against the counterclaim. Instead, the attorney will often require an upfront retainer to defend the creditor and charge their normal hourly fee. Unfortunately, this sometimes becomes a bone of contention and a misunderstanding between the creditor, collection agency, and the attorney.

The filing of counterclaims occurs more frequently on uncontested files. On a recent $10,000 file, after a fair amount of collection effort, the claim was subsequently placed with an attorney who accepted it within terms outlined previously. Within one month, a suit was filed and in less than three weeks a counterclaim was received in the amount of over $200,000 - asserting that the creditor breached a sole distributor contract with the debtor. Although the assertion was completely unsubstantiated and only an attempt to thwart the creditor's lawsuit, the creditor was in a position where he either had to: defend against the counter suit, offer to withdraw his claim and negotiate with the debtor to drop their counter claim, or try and strike an immediate monetary settlement.

The end result was that the creditor decided to fight the debtor's countersuit and after a few thousand dollars were spent on both sides, a settlement was reached, the debtor dropped their countersuit, and paid the creditor's account in full. Again, the countersuit was just a strategy by the debtor to maneuver out of the obligation to which the creditor was not prepared to accept and in this instance the fight paid off.

For the most part, a debtor will not pursue a countersuit against the creditor since this usually requires an hourly attorney's fee. If the reason they cannot pay the account in the first place is due to a lack of financial capability, then they most likely cannot afford to pay the hefty hourly fee charged by the attorney to pursue a counterclaim.

The main point here is that creditors should understand that costs incurred to defend a creditor in a counterclaim are not only additional to the cost of pursuing the original claim against the debtor, but that a counterclaim by the debtor is a strategy that some debtors may attempt to utilize to thwart the creditor's original claim. In addition, an experienced creditor's rights attorney should be selected in order to file a quick answer to a counterclaim and extinguish it before the debtor attempts to snuff out a legitimate debt.

How to Effectively Prepare for and Support the Litigation Process

Although the litigation process does not have to be complicated in the U.S. it can be challenging when the documentation and details required to support a claim are not well organized. Let's take a moment to review items that would greatly facilitate the litigation process, especially when the claim is quite large and is being disputed:

1. Think in terms of gathering all the documents from the time that the customer submitted the order to the point that the account was handed over to collection. In broad strokes the following documents are very important:

   - signed credit application
   - signed contract
   - signed purchase order
   - copies of packing slips and signed bills of lading
   - signed customer warehouse receipts
   - invoices
   - aging report
   - collection log

If these documents are available they will certainly help to substantiate the origination of the charges.

2. Submit only the "pertinent" emails or faxes that will reflect the discussion from point of order to the submission of the claim. The following emails are very helpful:

   - what has been ordered in quantity, model, type, etc. prior to the contract and purchase order
   - confirmation of delivery schedules and changes
   - disputes against the product or service and respective possible resolutions
   - indications or promises to pay or indications that payment will not be made

Sometimes we receive dozens of emails that don't apply to the reason(s) why the charges are not being paid. However, if you are unsure about the pertinence of an email, by all means feel free to send it on.

3. Set up a summary page of the documents that represent the time line of the transaction for which the claim is being litigated. The following fields are very helpful:

- date
- type of document (email, contract, fax, etc.)
- from
- to
- summary (especially when it comes to correspondence concerning disputes, please summarize the content)

When the documentation for the claim, especially a complicated one, comes well organized, not only can the third party collection effort commence quickly but should litigation of the claim become necessary, the attorney can proceed and be well prepared to substantiate the complaint more effectively.

Terms and Conditions of Sale, Part 1

Disputes, misunderstandings, accounts riddled with conflict and rising impatience – how do they start? Why does a supplier/customer relationship wither away from future sales and past profits lost, when it began with such promise?

Difficulties sometimes arise the moment the first order is processed, and without a strong foundation, the relationship will not be able to weather the adversity.

In terms of growing a beautiful garden, sales representatives plant the seeds, show the pretty picture to credit, and hope to harvest perennial commissions. Credit, order processing, shipping, compliance, cash application, and customer service tend to the daily tasks of nurturing. Expectations, assumptions and confusion are the enemies. Careful cultivation is the cure.

Many commercial creditors are revisiting their terms and conditions of sale, not just to review the content, but to clarify items such as:

- How clearly stated are the terms?
- How and when are they presented?
- What conditions must be present to allow for returns?
- What must be met for credits?
- Is there a provision requiring notification of a change in bank, ownership, and/or management?
- In other words, can a commercial creditor at least try to establish a foundation of understanding before weeds sprout?

FORM

Are the terms and conditions of the sale incorporated into the body of the credit application, on the back of the application, in a separate document, on the signed order form and/or disclosed in the purchase order confirmation prior to shipment?

If they do not appear above the customer's signature on the application, another signature is required, verifying the applicant's review and understanding. If certain terms and conditions only appear on the invoice, generated after the order, it's difficult to present a strong, credible argument that the customer understood, prior to the purchase, what was expected or the ramifications of late payment. Commercial collection agencies will not add collection fees or interest in excess of the state's legal rate (if indeed the debtor's state allows them at all) unless they are provided for in the terms and conditions, acknowledged by the customer's signature prior to the transaction.

If the terms and conditions are in a separate document, the signed copy is kept for the customer file, and another copy should be given to the customer for convenience, should it need to be referred to at a later time. It's not only a nice PR gesture, but offers excellent leverage if, after the account becomes delinquent, the customer suddenly claims the shipment was late or there was defective merchandise.

Are the term categories clearly indicated? A long document, with tiny print and continuous text may not be as well understood as short paragraphs that include emboldened headings (PRICING, GENERAL RETURNS, DEFECTIVE MERCHANDISE, PAYMENT POLICIES, etc.) to greatly help the customer read and understand the details of your terms and conditions.

Terms and Conditions of Sale, Part 2

CONTENT

What is most important for the customer to understand? What has been learned from previous customer conflicts? Are discounts allowed on closeouts and special promotions? Perhaps it's an important issue to address. No company can cover every exigency, but some of the most common policies included in the document, depending upon the creditor's industry, product, and procedures, are:

- terms on first orders (CIA, COD, credit card?)
- time allowance for application
- processing
- purchase orders
- pricing
- discounts
- minimum orders
- drop shipments
- order processing and fulfillment
- shipping procedures, carrier and charges
- back orders
- responsibility for assembly
- nsf charges/impact on credit line
- cancellations
- shortages and overages
- packing errors and damages
- general returns, return authorization and restocking charges
- notification of changes in ownership or management
- notification of changes in the entity organization (from and to)

    - sole proprietorship
    - limited partnership
    - limited liability company
    - limited liability partnership
    - corporation
    - force majeure

- terms of sale (including interest charged)
- the right to convert credit terms to credit card, CIA or COD at the vendor's discretion
- periodic credit reviews
- collection agency assignment
- collection fees and legal fees

PRESENTATION

If sales reps are familiar with the terms and conditions of a sale, they can be wonderful credit ambassadors by explaining the provisions in the same pleasant and winning way that captured the customer and sold the product. If they can leave a copy with the customer, it's perceived simply as an added service. If the terms and conditions are succinctly stated in boldly titled short paragraphs, everybody's on the same page – literally.

Sometimes, it's not possible for sales to be involved in the completion of the application or the introduction to the company policy. Then credit takes over as the liaison, providing the applicant with all the information needed to understand the rights and obligations as a customer, and to obtain all the information necessary to evaluate their financial stability.

Even if corporate or independent counsel creates the terms and conditions, credit and customer service should be included in the process. Not only do these two departments have insight into the most common difficulties, they often have a very direct way of phrasing the procedural cure. They speak the industry language and understand the customer's world.

After the applicant is approved, the terms and conditions can be provided, once again, either included in the body of a welcome letter or attached to it.

The Right of Set-Off
A Major Pitfall in the Suit Process

When a debtor has his funds in a bank account, at an institution to which he owes money, for example on a working capital loan, that institution may have the right under state law to seize any funds from the debtor's checking account, money market, or other related accounts and apply them to any of the debt that the debtor has with the financial institution. This is known as a "right of set-off."

About six months ago I received a claim from one of my clients, a logistics provider, who had a customer in central Texas for several years. Unfortunately, through circumstances out of his control, this customer fell into a very difficult financial situation and could not pay the $16,000 receivable balance due. Although the debtor had the will and volition to pay, he strongly insisted that he just did not have the capacity to pay all but about $300 per month.

Needless to say that after some short consultation with the creditor, we decided to hand the matter over to our attorney in Texas for further collection efforts. As our client kept very well organized and up to date records, we had the debtor's bank account and other very important documentation. Subsequently, it was necessary to pursue this claim through litigation and after only a few months, we received a default judgment.

Things were looking good and we were hoping that there would still be a significant amount of cash in the debtor's account to garnish and make this whole process a profitable endeavor. However, one of the pitfalls to trying to garnish a debtor's bank account is that the right to garnish any funds is subordinate to the right of the bank's set-off.

In our case, even though the funds in the debtor's bank account exceeded the $16,000 that was owed, the bank's right of set-off superseded our garnishment claim and unfortunately we could not seize any of the funds from the debtor's bank account. In addition, the bank had a lien on all of the debtor's remaining receivables as well as the movable assets. In other words, we hit a legal brick wall and there was nothing more we could do.

Fortunately, the debtor did not dismiss his obligation and even with all of the legal difficulties, he still maintained a desire to pay off the debt as best as he could, and has been doing so for the past few months.

For the most part, the litigation process through to judgment, and the ability to garnish funds in a debtor's bank has worked successfully countless times in the past. However, there's still no crystal ball as to any number of twists, turns and surprises (and the right of set-offs) that can thwart all of our good efforts to try and recover what is rightfully yours.

The Uniform Commercial Code (UCC) and What It Means to Your Business

By the National Association of Equipment Dealers Association

The Uniform Commercial Code (UCC) is a law enacted in all 50 states to regulate commercial transactions. Article 9 of the UCC allows for a public notice (UCC-1) to be filed in a designated state filing office by dealers (or lenders) to perfect their security interests in equipment that is bought and/or financed. The UCC-1 filing is valid for five years and can be continued to extend the financing statement for additional terms of five years. Filing is usually with the office of the Secretary of State in the state of residence, incorporation or business formation.

Why you need to know about the UCC law

As a buyer and/or a seller of equipment, you need to protect yourself and your business from potential losses because of outstanding equipment liens.

How to check for a UCC-1 filing:

- Conduct a UCC search with the office of the Secretary of State or other agency responsible for UCC filings in your state.

- Generally, you only need to perform a search in the state where the customer is located or resides using the customer's correct legal name and the following rules:

    - Individual: Search the state where the customer resides.

    - Corporation, LLC, Limited Partnership: Search in the state where the business is incorporated or organized.

    - General Partnership: Search in the state where the partnership has its principal place of business and in the state(s) where its general partners reside.

Existing Liens:

If a lien is specific to a piece of equipment involved in a trade, require the customer to pay off the lien before the sale or trade, or have the lien paid off simultaneously with the sale.

If the lien is a blanket lien, obtain a written release from the bank (the secured party) on the equipment. A release can be as simple as one sentence. Banks will generally consent because its customer is getting replacement collateral with equity available to the bank that is equal to the value of the trade-in.

Correct legal name
Individuals or sole proprietors:

- Whether an individual or sole proprietor, always identify customers by their correct legal names.

- Never use trade names or d/b/a.

- Ask the customer for a valid driver's license, birth certificate, Social Security card or other form of identification. Requesting this type of documentation may seem impractical, but it's the best way to ensure that your dealership obtains a customer's correct legal name.

- Failing to search or file a UCC-1 with the correct legal name may cause you to overlook liens or lose the perfected status of your security interest and priority over others.

Corporation, Limited Liability Co. (LLC), Limited Partnership:

- Use the name on the Articles of Incorporation or equivalent filed with the state of incorporation or organization, typically the office of Secretary of State.

- Debtor says the name of his/her company is Doe Farms, Inc., a Kansas corporation. But when you check with the Secretary of State, the office identifies the debtor company as Doe Family Farms, Inc. Use the Doe Family Farms, Inc. in your searches and filings.

- Contact the appropriate state agency to identify the correct legal name. Obtaining a copy of the Articles of Incorporation and all amendments to those articles is the safe choice.

General Partnership:

- General Partnerships (GP's) are not registered organizations in most states. GP's are registered organizations in California and the option of filing organization documents in some other states is allowed.

- The correct name of a General Partnership is the name identified on its organization document or partnership agreement.

- Ask the debtor to see the partnership agreement to confirm that the correct legal name is used.

- The best practice is to search and file under the names of all the general partners in addition to the partnership name.

Customer name changes

When a customer (debtor on which you have filed a UCC-1) changes its name (generally corporations or limited liability companies) or when a person or organization purchases all the debtor's assets or succeeds to all its liabilities and becomes a new debtor, you should:

- File an amendment to the original UCC-1 for a pure name change, e.g., Doe Farms, Inc. changes its name to Doe Family Farms, Inc.

- File a new UCC-1 if another person or organization becomes a new debtor, e.g., Doe Family Farms, Inc. purchases Smith Farms, Inc.

If you fail to file an amendment or original UCC-1 to reflect the name change, it is not considered a perfected security interest in any collateral acquired beyond four months of the change. In doing lien searches, use both old and new correct legal names.

Customer location changes

If a customer/debtor changes location, i.e., an individual moves across state lines or a general partnership moves its principal place of business to another state, your financing statement is in effect for whichever of the following time periods occur first:

- four months after the debtor changes location, or
- the original financing statement lapses

Then you should file a new UCC-1.

If you fail to file a new UCC-1 in the new location within the time periods previously mentioned, your security interest is deemed unperfected and loses its effectiveness to any subsequent purchaser for value.

Equipment is transferred / moved to another location
If your customer/debtor transfers equipment to a third party, your security interest stays with the equipment unless you consent to the transfer free of the security interest. The consent and release should be in writing.

However, if a third party is located in another state, your financing statement is in effect for whichever of the following time periods occurs first:

- one year after the transfer and change in location, or
- the original financing statement lapses

Then you should file a new UCC-1.

If you fail to file a new UCC-1 in the new location within the time periods previously mentioned, your security interest is deemed unperfected and loses its effectiveness to any subsequent purchaser.

Where to file a UCC-1 statement:

- If your customer is an individual or sole proprietor, always file it with the state where the customer resides using the customer's correct legal name.

- If your customer is a corporation, always file it with the state where the corporation is incorporated using the customer's correct legal name.

- If your customer is a limited liability company (LLC), always file it with the state where the LLC is organized using the customer's correct legal name.

The best ways to protect yourself:

- Always conduct a UCC search.
- Always use the correct legal name on the UCC-1.
- Always ask the customer about existing liens.
- Always pay attention to changes affecting the security interest.

Recommended best practices for your dealership
UCC process for financing a transaction:

- name verification
- ucc search
- federal & state tax lien
- pending suits and judgments
- ucc filing
- search to reflect
- monitor and track it

UCC process for not financing a transaction:

- name verification
- ucc search

Corporation Service Company (CSC) provided information in this summary. CSC • 2711 Centerville Rd., Wilmington, DE 19808 • (302) 636-5400 •https://www.incspot.com

The Uniform Commercial Code (UCC) & What It Means to Your Business NORTH AMERICAN EQUIPMENT DEALERS ASSOCIATION • 1195 Smizer Mill Road, Fenton, MO63026 • Phone: (636) 349-5000 • Fax: (636) 349-5443 • www.naeda.com

What Happens After Judgment

The Situation: The creditor has prevailed and judgment has been granted. Post judgment interest, a reimbursement of court costs expended by the creditor and "reasonable" attorney fees (determined by the court) may, at the court's discretion, be included in the award.

The Possibilities: The debtor may pay in full or offer an acceptable payment plan or settlement. The issue is either resolved or in the process of resolution. Upon fulfillment, the debtor is released from indebtedness; the judgment is recorded as satisfied.

If the debtor shows no sign of cooperation, demonstrates no willingness, or claims no capacity to address the issue, the creditor may employ post judgment collection rights allowed by law.

The Challenges: As the laws governing the execution of judgments are statutory, post judgment collection rights and remedies vary from state to state. In some instances, there are variances between different courts within a state. The need for knowledgeable legal representation, experienced in commercial law, far from ending at the award of judgment, remains critical in the post judgment stage.

Rights and Remedies: The first inconsistency is evident the moment the judgment is entered into the court records. Some state statutes mandate a specific period of time, a period of grace, to elapse before execution may be attempted. In other states the Clerk of Court issues execution automatically when the judgment is entered.

The Writ of Execution: This is the decree or order of the court, usually petitioned for by creditor's counsel and issued by the clerk, instructing the sheriff (constable or marshal in some jurisdictions) to seize the defendant's eligible property to satisfy the judgment. The Writ, however, does not include real property. The creation of a lien on real property is a process that, again, varies from state to state.

The Levy: This is the actual process by which an officer of the court takes possession of the debtor's eligible and identified property. The custody is termed the "attachment." After allowing the debtor the prescribed notice, the property is sold at public auction and the net proceeds, after sheriff's fees, are remitted to creditor's counsel. Any excess funds are returned to the debtor.

The time allowed for execution and levy will also vary from state to state. Should counsel require additional court costs to initiate and complete the process, the creditor should provide the funds as quickly as possible.

What if no attachable assets are found

The Situation: The debtor has failed to satisfy the judgment voluntarily and the execution has come back empty. The judgment appears a hollow victory.

The Possibilities: Allowing again for statutory differences and procedural diversity, judgment creditors have the right to supplementary proceedings.

The Debtor Examination: By order or subpoena, a judgment debtor (or others who may be appropriately connected and ostensibly knowledgeable) may be directed to appear before the court or a referee, for an examination under oath, by creditor's counsel. The debtor examination may well reveal hidden assets or, possibly, a fraudulent transfer of assets.

Discovery: Interrogatories, instruments of discovery usually associated with the first stages of litigation can be equally useful in the post judgment environment. A cost effective and efficient tool especially if employed promptly, the completed document may well identify, as well as qualify, attachable assets.

Deposition: A deposition, although expensive, is also powerful, as it allows direct questioning under oath and a written transcript.

What if there is no clear, simple avenue to attachable assets

The Situation: The judgment is against the personal guarantor, sole proprietor, or general partner and the debtor entity. A sizable debt owed to the debtor or debtor entity is discovered, the individual is found to have steady employment elsewhere or the debtor and/or debtor entity is found to hold title to real property.

The Possibilities:

1. **Garnishment:** Although hardly uniform in terms, latitude, and procedure, the right to attach to debtor's property held by a third party, or to capture funds owed to the debtor by a third party is accorded creditors by almost every state. Throughout much of New England, it is termed a "trustee process," in Pennsylvania and New Jersey it is called a "judgment execution." Whatever the term, the process is subject to state statute, and state law strictly defines the extent of the creditor's rights.

2. **Wage Garnishment:** Also known as income execution and wage attachment, a claim on a debtor's wages is governed by federal law, under the Consumer Credit Protection Act. If a state's wage garnishment law is construed in favor of the debtor, the more restrictive law will probably rule. The creditor's attorney will offer to assess the recovery potential and decide if a wage garnishment is a cost effective tool.

3. **Liens on Real Property:** Every state has specific statutes governing the creation of lien status and unless a creditor deals exclusively in one state, there will be exposure to many permutations of the same basic right: the ability to register a claim on the debtor's real property and establish priority over subsequently docketed judgments and unsecured creditors. Rarely does the entry of a judgment create a lien. In most states, there are prescribed procedures and additional filings, especially if there is property in another country. The life of a real property lien also

varies widely. In Florida, a lien is effective for 7 years, but may be extended to 20; in California, it is effective for 10 years; in the District of Columbia, for 12 years; in Ohio, 5 years.

What if property is jointly held

Most states prohibit liens on property not held solely in the debtor's name. Some such as California, Louisiana, Nevada, New Mexico and Washington do allow liens on property held by husband and wife. The creditor's attorney will always advise the appropriate and most effective strategy for securing interest in all assets.

What if a judgment is awarded in one state, but has to be enforced in another

By virtue of the selection of forum and choice of law in the terms and conditions of sale, or simply by choice, the creditor may elect to sue the debtor in the creditor's state jurisdiction (a long arm suit) and "domesticate" the judgment in the debtor's jurisdiction. Perhaps, after judgment, assets are discovered in another state. Whatever the reason, there is a Constitutional doctrine of "full faith and credit," which provides for acceptance, by the courts of one state, of another state's judgment. There are, however, a few stumbling blocks. An exemplified copy of the judgment (certified by judge and clerk) must be obtained, new counsel engaged in the new venue, at added expense, and, should the debtor engage counsel to oppose, the new action must be defended. A number of states have adopted the Uniform Judgment Act, which simplifies the process, but it has not become universal.

Can the debtor exempt assets

All states allow a judgment debtor homestead and/or personal property exemption, providing qualified immunity from execution and levy. Some statutes are quite generous, others, highly restrictive.

Concluding Thoughts

This book is the first of several that I plan to publish. Future books will contain reprinted and additional selected articles from up and coming newsletters that I feel will be of particular importance to credit professionals.

Like all of our publications, your comments and feedback will continue to encourage the publishing of material of value and is always appreciated.

As future books are a work in progress, your thoughts, ideas, and opinions (at my email address below) on this book as well as those being developed, will go a long way in refining the finished product.

Copies of this book can be purchased from Amazon.com. In addition, special discounts are available when purchased in bulk for premiums and sales promotions as well as for fund-raising or educational use. Special editions or book excerpts can also be created to specification. For details contact me by phone or at the email address below.

I look forward to hearing from you.

Sincerely,

Lou Figueroa
President

Credit Decisions International, Ltd.
Phone: 800.922.9688
Fax: 800.972.3328
lfigueroa@creditdecisions.com
http://www.creditdecisions.com
http://www.creditbytes.blogspot.com